A PROPHET'S
VOICE

INSPIRING QUOTES FROM
JOSEPH SMITH

A PROPHET'S
VOICE

INSPIRING QUOTES FROM
JOSEPH SMITH

ED J. PINEGAR

Covenant Communications, Inc.

Covenant

Published by Covenant Communications, Inc.
American Fork, Utah

Printed in Canada
First Printing: May 2005

11 10 09 08 07 06 05   10 9 8 7 6 5 4 3 2 1

ISBN 1-59156-973-7

TABLE OF CONTENTS

SOURCES AND ABBREVIATIONS

A of F   Articles of Faith

D&C   Doctrine and Covenants

JS—H   Joseph Smith—History

JD   *Journal of Discourses.*

Lectures   *Lectures on Faith.* 1985.

                Andrus, Hyrum L., & Helen Mae
                Andrus. *They Knew the Prophet.* 2004.

Discourses   Burton, Alma P., comp. *Discourses of
                the Prophet Joseph Smith.* 1985.

                Cannon, George Q. *The Life of Joseph
                Smith, the Prophet.* 1986.

Encyclopedia Dahl, Larry E., & Donald Q. Cannon,
                ed. *Encyclopedia of Joseph Smith's
                Teachings.* 2000.

                Ehat, Andrew F. & Lyndon W. Cook.,
                comp. *The Words of Joseph Smith: The
                Contemporary Accounts of the Nauvoo
                Discourses of the Prophet Joseph.* 1991.

Commentary   Jackson, Kent P., comp. and ed. *Joseph
                Smith's Commentary on the Bible.* 1994.

Writings   Jessee, Dean C., comp. *The Personal
                Writings of Joseph Smith.* 1984.

Madsen, Truman G. *Joseph Smith the Prophet.* 1990.

HC   Roberts, B. H., comp. and ed. *History of the Church.* 1976–80.

————. *Joseph Smith, the Prophet-Teacher.* 1967.

TPJS   Smith, Joseph Fielding, comp. *Teachings of the Prophet Joseph Smith.* 2002.

Unless otherwise noted, original punctuation and spelling has been used.

THE PROPHET

As a young boy, I was fascinated with and in awe of the Prophet Joseph. He became my mortal hero. He was more than a man. He was a prophet of God—the prophet of the Restoration—and it all began when he was but a boy of fourteen. Accounts describe him as righteous and sober-minded in his youth, yet with a nature of familiarity and friendliness. Like Mormon and Moroni in the Book of Mormon, he was called of God early in his life, and through him, Christ restored the truths of the gospel and revealed the word of God that we might have the very word of God to live by (see D&C 84:44).

My testimony of Joseph Smith was strengthened years later when I was teaching the Book of Mormon at BYU. I had the opportunity one day to speak with President Harold B. Lee. After receiving some advice as to how to improve my teaching of the scriptures, I thanked him and told him how I loved and sustained him as a prophet. He then shared his testimony with me of the prophet Joseph Smith. As he bore that sacred and solemn testimony, it was burned into my soul. I had known Joseph was a prophet, but now I had

3

a fervent testimony of the prophet of the Restoration.

Indeed, the Prophet Joseph was a mighty prophet of God, for the Heavens were open to him as the Restoration unfolded in these the latter days. Brigham Young said of the Prophet Joseph Smith: "It was decreed in the counsels of eternity, long before the foundations of the earth were laid, that he should be the man, in the last dispensation of this world, to bring forth the word of God to the people, and receive the fulness of the keys and power of the Priesthood of the Son of God" (Daniel H. Ludlow, "A Tribute to Joseph Smith, Jr.," *The Prophet Joseph: Essays on the Life and Mission of Joseph Smith,* 1988, 337).

Following Joseph's martyrdom, John Taylor recorded this testimony of him:

> Joseph Smith, the Prophet and Seer of the Lord, has done more, save Jesus only, for the salvation of men in this world, than any other man that ever lived in it. In the short space of twenty years, he has brought forth the Book of Mormon, which he translated by the gift and power of God, and has been the means of publishing it on two continents; has sent the fulness of the everlasting gospel, which it contained, to the four quarters of the earth; has brought forth the revelations and commandments which compose this book of Doctrine

and Covenants, and many other wise documents and instructions for the benefit of the children of men; gathered many thousands of the Latter-day Saints, founded a great city, and left a fame and name that cannot be slain. He lived great, and he died great in the eyes of God and his people. (D&C 135:3–4)

It wasn't only members of the Church who felt the importance of Joseph's influence on mankind. Josiah Quincy, mayor of Boston from 1845 to 1849, visited the Prophet in Nauvoo in May 1844. He was so impressed with Joseph, he held him in the same esteem as other eminent Americans such as John Adams, Daniel Webster, and Andrew Jackson and recorded the following:

It is by no means improbable that some future textbook for the use of generations yet unborn, will contain a question something like this: What historical American of the nineteenth century has exerted the most powerful influence upon the destinies of his countrymen? And it is by no means impossible that the answer to that interrogatory may be thus written: Joseph Smith, the Mormon Prophet, And the reply, absurd as it doubtless seems to most men now living, may be an obvious commonplace to their descendants. History deals in surprises and paradoxes quite as startling as this. The man who established a religion in this age of free debate, who was and is today accepted by hundreds of thousands as a direct emissary from the Most High,—such a rare human being is not to be disposed of by pelting his memory with unsavory epithets. (B. H. Roberts, A Comprehensive History of the Church, 1991, 2:349–50)

Now, as we approach the bicentennial of Joseph Smith's birth, my thoughts are turned to the words and teachings of the prophet of the Restoration. It seems there is nothing that Joseph did not address. In fact, John Henry Evan, a biographer of Joseph Smith, has commented that

Nothing was too trivial or too big to occupy his thoughts. He talked about tea, coffee, and tobacco; about the hours one should sleep and work; about whether the human epidermis changes every seven years; about laying out a city that would give a town and a country effect in one; about how to eliminate both poverty and riches from our present economic system; about the arrogance of those who come into power too soon; about the "planet that is nearest the throne of God"; about the much mooted question of his day as to whether the earth and man were created out of nothing or out of pre-existing matter; about the freedom of the will; about heaven and hell and whether there is a devil; about God and the true immortality of the soul. (Joseph Smith, an American Prophet, 1989, 10)

Of course, the power of Joseph Smith's words was strongest when he testified of the Restoration and expounded on the scriptures. Parley P. Pratt records an incident in 1839 when Joseph and Sidney Rigdon, along with others, were invited to speak to a large group in Philadelphia. Sidney was the first to address the congregation, and in fear of offending the people present, he spoke academically of the Church and the restoration of the gospel, defending it with passages from the Bible but avoiding references to the miraculous events of the Restoration. Such timidity annoyed the Prophet. Parley records that

> When he [Sidney Rigdon] was through, brother Joseph arose like a lion about to roar; and being full of the Holy Ghost, spoke in great power, bearing testimony of the visions he had seen, the ministering of angels which he had enjoyed; and how he had found the plates of the Book of Mormon, and translated them by the gift and power of God. He commenced by saying: 'If nobody else had the courage to testify of so glorious a record, he felt to do it in justice to the people, and leave the event with God.'
>
> The entire congregation were astounded; electrified, as it were, and overwhelmed with the sense of the truth and power by which he spoke, and the wonders which he related. A lasting impression was made; many souls

were gathered into the fold. And I bear witness, that he, by his faithful and powerful testimony, cleared his garments of their blood.
(in Joseph Fielding McConkie, *Seeking the
Spirit,* 1978, 42–44)

When Joseph preached and taught, he didn't
do so in the trained style of the orators of his day.
His was a unique style, one which seamlessly
merged his personality with his divine calling.
Parley Pratt describes it as follows:

His manner was easy and familiar . . . and
his language abounding in original eloquence peculiar to himself—not polished—
not studied—not smoothed and softened by
education and refined by art; but flowing
forth in its own native simplicity, and pro-
fusely abounding in variety of subject and
manner. He interested and edified, while, at
the same time, he amused and entertained
his audience; and none listened to him that
were ever weary with his discourse. I have
even known him to retain a congregation of
willing and anxious listeners for many hours
together, in the midst of cold or sunshine,
rain or wind, while they were laughing at one
moment and weeping the next. Even his
most bitter enemies were generally overcome, if he could once get their ears. (in
Joseph Fielding McConkie, Seeking the
Spirit, 1978, 42–44)

Wandle Mace testified of the power of the Prophet's teaching.

> I have listened to the Prophet Joseph in public, and in private, in sun shine and shower, as many others have done, as he taught from the stand, At my own house, and at his house, I have been familiar with him, from the time he escaped from prison in Missouri and reached Quincy Illinois in 1839 until his Martyrdom on June 27th 1844, and do know that no man could explain the scripture, throw them wide open to view, so plain that none could mis understand their meaning, *except he had been taught of God.*
>
> I have felt sometimes ashamed of myself, having studied the scriptures so much, that I had not seen that which was so plain when he touched them. He as it were, turned the key, and the door of knowledge sprang wide open, disclosing precious principles, both new and old. I have many times been pondering upon a subject, and seemed to come to a stand still, not knowing how to gain farther information relating to it, when upon going to meeting on the sabbath, the key—as it were—would be touched by Joseph and the subject would be so plain I wondered why I had not seen it before. (*Autobiography,* 1890, 34)

Brigham Young went on to describe the effect of Joseph's style further:

When I saw Joseph Smith, he took heaven, figuratively speaking, and brought it down to earth; and he took the earth, brought it up, and opened up, in plainness and simplicity, the things of God. The excellency of the glory of the character of Brother Joseph Smith was that he could reduce heavenly things to the understanding of the finite. When he preached to the people—revealed the things of God, the will of God, the plan of salvation, the purposes of Jehovah, the relation in which we stand to Him and all the heavenly beings—he reduced his teachings to the capacity of every man, woman, and child, making them as plain as a well-defined pathway. This should have convinced every person that ever heard of him of his divine authority and power, for no other man was able to teach as he could, and no person can reveal the things of God, but by the revelations of Jesus Christ. (Hyrum L. Andrus and Helen Mae Andrus, *They Knew the Prophet*, 2004, 34–35)

Truly, we are blessed today to have the teachings of a prophet of God who taught in such a manner that we might all understand the doctrines of the gospel. It is my prayer as you read this book that you might be touched by the power, eloquence, and power of Joseph Smith's words as much as I have. Clearly, everything that

Joseph has said cannot be included in a book of this sort, as his teachings fill volumes, but the quotes that have been included provide a brief glimpse and reminder of the power of the voice of a prophet.

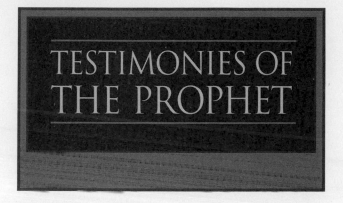

TESTIMONIES OF
THE PROPHET

BRIGHAM YOUNG

I honor and revere the name of Joseph Smith. I delight to hear it; I love it. I love his doctrine. (*Discourses of Brigham Young*, 1954, 458)

I feel like shouting Hallelujah, all the time, when I think that I ever knew Joseph Smith, the Prophet whom the Lord raised up and ordained, and to whom he gave keys and power to build up the Kingdom of God on earth and sustain it. These keys are committed to this people, and we have power to continue the work that Joseph commenced, until everything is prepared for the coming of the Son of Man. (*Discourses of Brigham Young*, 1954, 458)

Who can justly say aught against Joseph Smith? I was as well acquainted with him, as any man. . . . And I am bold to say that, Jesus Christ excepted, no better man ever lived or does live upon this earth. I am his witness. (*Discourses of Brigham Young*, 1954, 459)

All that Joseph Smith did was to preach the truth—the Gospel as the Lord revealed it to him—and tell the people how to be saved, and the honest-in-heart ran together and gathered around him and loved him as they did their own lives. He could do no more than to preach true principles, and that will gather the Saints in the last days, even the honest-in-heart. All who believe and obey the Gospel of Jesus Christ are his witnesses to the truth of these statements. (*Discourses of Brigham Young,* 1954, 463)

JOHN TAYLOR

I testify that I was acquainted with Joseph Smith for years. I have traveled with him; I have been with him in private and in public; I have associated with him in councils of all kinds; I have listened hundreds of times to his public teachings, and his advice to his friends and associates of a more private nature. I have been at his house and seen his deportment in his family. I have seen him arraigned before the tribunals of his country, and have seen him honorably acquitted, and delivered from the pernicious breath of slander, and the machinations and falsehoods of wicked and corrupt men. I was with him living, and with him when he died, when he was murdered in

Carthage jail by a ruthless mob . . . with their faces painted. . . . I have seen him, then, under these various circumstances, and I testify before God, angels, and men, that he was a good, honorable, virtuous man—that his doctrines were good, scriptural, and wholesome—that his precepts were such as became a man of God—that his private and public character was unimpeachable—and that he lived and died as a man of God and a gentleman. This is my testimony. (Mark H. Taylor, ed. *Witness to the Martyrdom: John Taylor's Personal Account of the Last Days of the Prophet Joseph Smith,* 1999, 155–56)

If I did not believe that Joseph Smith was a true prophet, I should not have been here. If he was a true prophet, and spake the word of the Lord, that is just as binding on the human family as any other word spoken by any other prophet. The scriptures tell us that "Man shall not live by bread alone, but by every word that proceedeth out of the mouth of God." (Matthew 4:4) . . . Gentlemen, I again say that Joseph Smith was a virtuous, high-minded, honorable man, a gentleman and a Christian. But he introduced principles which strike at the root of the corrupt systems of men. This necessarily comes in contact with their prepossessions, prejudices, and interests; and as they cannot overturn his principles, they attack his character. And that is one reason why we have so many books written against his character, without touching his principles, and also why we meet with so much opposition. But truth, eternal truth, is invulnerable. It cannot be destroyed, but like the throne of Jehovah, it will outride all the storms of men, and live for ever. (*The Gospel Kingdom: Selections from the Writings and Discourses of John Taylor,* 1987, 356)

WILFORD WOODRUFF

It has been my faith and belief from the time that I was made acquainted with the gospel that no greater prophet than Joseph Smith ever lived on the face of the earth save Jesus Christ. He was raised up to stand at the head of this great dispensation—the greatest of all dispensations God has ever given to man. He remarked on several occasions when conversing with his brethren: "Brethren, you do not know me, you do not know who I am." (*The Discourses of Wilford Woodruff,* 1969, 43)

I had a great desire in my boyhood to receive the Gospel of Christ, to see a prophet or somebody that could teach me the Gospel of Christ as taught by the ancient Apostles and as I read of in the New

Testament. . . . I was in Zion's Camp with the Prophet of God. I saw the dealings of God with him. I saw the power of God with him. I saw that he was a Prophet. What was manifest to him by the power of God upon that mission was of great value to me and to all who received his instructions. (In Conference Report, Apr. 1898, 29)

The last speech that Joseph Smith ever made to the quorum of the Apostles was in a building in Nauvoo, and it was such a speech as I never heard from mortal man before or since. He was clothed upon with the Spirit and power of God. His face was clear as amber. The room was filled as with consuming fire. He stood three hours upon his feet. Said he: "You Apostles of the Lamb of God have been chosen to carry out the purposes of the Lord on the earth. Now, I have received, as the Prophet, seer and revelator, standing at the head of this dispensation, every key, every ordinance, every principle and every Priesthood that belongs to the last dispensation and fulness of times. And I have sealed all these things upon your heads. Now, you Apostles, if you do not rise up and bear off this kingdom, as I have given it to you, you will be damned."

I am the only witness left on earth that can bear record of this, and I am thankful that I have lived to see the day in which I stand. . . . I feel to thank God that I have lived as long as I have, and to see as much as I have in fulfillment of the words of the Prophet of God. (In Conference Report, Apr. 1898, 89–90)

LORENZO SNOW

A word or two about Joseph Smith. Perhaps there are very few men now living who were so well acquainted with Joseph Smith the Prophet as I was. I was with him oftentimes. I visited with him in his family, sat at his table, associated with him under various circumstances, and had private interviews with him for counsel. I know that Joseph Smith was a prophet of God; I know that he was an honorable man, a moral man, and that he had the respect of those who were acquainted with him. The Lord has shown me most clearly and completely that he was a prophet of God, and that he held the holy priesthood. (*The Teachings of Lorenzo Snow*, 1984, 55)

Joseph Smith, the Prophet, with whom I was intimately acquainted for years, as well as I was with my brother, I know him to have been a man of integrity, a man devoted to the interests of humanity and to the requirements of God all the days in which he was permitted to live. There never was a man that possessed a higher degree of integrity and more devotedness to the interest of mankind than the Prophet Joseph Smith. I can say this from a personal acquaintance with him. (In Conference Report, Apr. 1898, 64)

JOSEPH F. SMITH

Joseph Smith was a true prophet of God. He lived and died a true prophet, and his words and works will yet demonstrate the divinity of his mission to millions of the inhabitants of this globe. Perhaps not so many that are now living, for they have in a great measure rejected the gospel, and the testimony which the elders of this Church have borne to them; but their children after them, and generations to come, will receive with delight the name of the Prophet Joseph Smith, and the gospel which their fathers rejected. (*Gospel Doctrine: Selections from the Sermons and Writings of Joseph F. Smith*, 1978, 485–86)

To me it is very strange indeed that there should be so much extreme ill feeling manifested by the world against Joseph Smith. He wronged no man. I am a witness of that, for I know his life. I have seen him in the flesh, and I have read of his sayings. I have read the revelations that the Lord gave to him. I am familiar with his work, and I know that he never wronged a living soul. He did not injure his fellowmen, but he did much to exalt them. (*Proceedings at the Dedication of the Joseph Smith Memorial Monument: At Sharon, Windsor County, Vermont, December 23rd, 1905,* 41)

HEBER J. GRANT

Joseph Smith was and is a prophet of the true and the living God. Joseph Smith was the instrument in the hands of God of establishing upon the earth the true gospel of the Lord Jesus Christ. (*Gospel Standards: Selections from the Sermons and Writings of Heber J. Grant,* 1969, 180)

The day can never come when we will do that [eliminate Joseph Smith from our teachings]. As well might we undertake to leave out Jesus Christ, the Son of the living God. Either Joseph Smith did see God and did converse with Him, and God Himself did introduce Jesus Christ to the boy Joseph Smith, and Jesus Christ did tell Joseph Smith that he would be the instrument in the hands of God of establishing again upon the earth the true gospel of Jesus Christ—or Mormonism, so-called, is a myth. And Mormonism is not a myth! It is the power of God unto salvation. (*Gospel Standards: Selections from the Sermons and Writings of Heber J. Grant,* 1969, 3)

I know that God lives. I know that Jesus is the Christ. I know that Joseph Smith was a prophet of God. . . . I know that God chose His prophet Joseph Smith and gave him instructions and authority to establish this work, and that the power and the influence of Joseph Smith are now being felt as the angel promised. His name is known for good or evil all over the world, but for evil only by those who malign him. Those who know him, those who know his teachings, know his life was pure and that his teachings were in very deed God's law. (In Conference Report, Apr. 1943, 7–8)

GEORGE ALBERT SMITH

Much has been said in this conference about the Prophet Joseph Smith. There isn't much that I could say, except that which is good. Many of the benefits and blessings that have come to me have come through that man who gave his life for the gospel of Jesus Christ. There have been some who have belittled him, but I would like to say that those who have done so will be forgotten and their remains will go back to mother earth, if they have not already gone, and the odor of their infamy will never die, while the glory and honor and majesty and courage and fidelity manifested by the Prophet Joseph Smith will attach to his name forever. (In Conference Report, Apr. 1946, 181–82)

I could, if I had time, open to you the Doctrine and Covenants containing the prophecies, the revelations of God to the Prophet Joseph Smith, and show that one by one they have been fulfilled, not by Joseph Smith's power but by the power of God. . . . While Joseph Smith might write those words [D&C 89:18–19], he couldn't fulfil that promise. (In Conference Report, Apr. 1945, 21)

I know that God lives. I know that Jesus is the Christ. I know that Joseph Smith was a prophet of the living God, as I know that I stand here and talk to you. (*The Teachings of George Albert Smith*, 1996, 29)

DAVID O. McKAY

When Joseph Smith taught a doctrine, he taught it authoritatively. His was not the question whether it agreed with man's thoughts or not, whether it was in harmony with the teachings of the orthodox churches or whether it was in direct opposition. What was given to him he gave to the world irrespective of its agreement or disagreement, of its harmony or its discord with the belief of the churches, or the prevailing standards of mankind; and today, as we look through the vista of over one hundred years, we have a good opportunity of judging of the virtue of his teachings, and of concluding as to the source of his instruction. . . .

Each succeeding year of the past century has tended to vindicate, and the contending creeds of Christendom today confirm, the Prophet's teachings in regard to the necessity of divine authority to officiate in the things pertaining to God.

Not only did he receive guidance and instruction from the divine Head, but, once received, defended it with invincible resolution, and his "reliance on truth, on virtue and in God were most unfaltering." (*Gospel Ideals: Selections from the Discourses of David O. McKay,* 1953, 81–82)

The Prophet Joseph Smith, but a youth, did not argue upon the personality of God; he did not speculate upon that eternal source of energy and intelligence from which all life gets its being; he merely stated the truth. (*Gospel Ideals: Selections from the Discourses of David O. McKay,* 1953, 22)

I know that the gospel was restored through the Prophet Joseph Smith, by the Father and the Son, who are as real today in connection with the other world as my loved one and yours. (*Gospel Ideals: Selections from the Discourses of David O. McKay,* 1953, 84)

JOSEPH FIELDING SMITH

I am thankful for the restoration of eternal truth in this final gospel dispensation; for the mission and ministry of Joseph Smith, the Prophet, . . . and for the fact that the keys of the kingdom of God have been committed again to man on the earth. ("A Prophet's Blessing," *Ensign,* July 1972, 130)

I know that the Father and the Son appeared to the Prophet Joseph Smith to usher in this final gospel dispensation.

I know that Joseph Smith was and is a prophet. ("Let the Spirit of Oneness Prevail," *Ensign,* Dec. 1971, 136)

HAROLD B. LEE

When finally we get that one divine thought that Joseph Smith was and is a prophet and that the gospel is true, all the other seeming difficulties melt away like heavy frost before the coming of the rising sun. . . .

As one of the humblest among us, and from the depths of my soul, I too want to add my humble testimony. I know that Joseph Smith was a prophet of the living God. I know that he lived and died to bring to this generation the means by which salvation could be gained. I know that he sits in a high place and holds the keys of this last dispensation. I know that for those who follow him and listen to his teachings and accept him as a true prophet of God and his revelations and teachings as the word of God, the gates of hell will not prevail against them.

No man can accept Jesus Christ as the Savior of the world, no man can accept this as His church, the Church of Jesus Christ, unless he can accept Joseph Smith as God's mouthpiece and the restorer of His work in these latter days. First, to say that we are Christians then requires two or three certainties. We must know for certainty in our hearts and minds that Jesus is the Christ, the Savior of the world. We must know that this is indeed the Church of Jesus Christ, the kingdom of God on earth in these last days; and finally we must have a testimony that Joseph Smith was a prophet of God. (*The Teachings of Harold B. Lee,* 1996, 134, 371)

SPENCER W. KIMBALL

Joseph Smith is a true prophet of the living God and his successors likewise. (*Faith Precedes the Miracle,* 1975, 328)

I am grateful for the Prophet Joseph Smith, born in this month so many years ago. We do not need the world to tell us how wonderful the Prophet Joseph Smith was. ("A Gift of Gratitude," *Tambuli,* Dec. 1977, 1)

Knowing full well that before long, in the natural course of events, I must stand before the Lord and give an accounting of my words, I now add my personal and solemn testimony that God, the Eternal Father, and the risen Lord, Jesus Christ, appeared to the boy Joseph Smith. I testify that the Book of Mormon is a translation of an ancient record of nations who once lived in this western hemisphere . . .

I testify that the holy priesthood, both Aaronic and Melchizedek, with authority to act in the name of God, was restored to the earth by John the Baptist, and Peter, James, and John; that other keys and authority were subsequently restored; and that the power and authority of those various divine bestowals are among us today. Of these things I bear solemn witness to all within the sound of my voice. ("Remarks and Dedication of the Fayette, New York, Buildings," *Ensign,* May 1980, 54)

EZRA TAFT BENSON

The faith of members of The Church of Jesus Christ of Latter-day Saints rests on the claim that Joseph Smith is a prophet of God. . . .

Was Joseph Smith sent from God? We answer an emphatic yes! . . .

I testify to you that God has again spoken from the heavens; that the visitation of God the Father and his Son Jesus Christ constitutes the greatest event in this world since the resurrection of Jesus Christ. . . .

I bear testimony that Joseph Smith was a prophet of the living God, one of the greatest prophets that has ever lived on the earth. He was the instrument in God's hand in ushering in the present gospel dispensation, the greatest of all, and the last of all in preparation for the second coming of the Master. ("Joseph Smith: Prophet to Our Generation," *Ensign,* Mar. 1994, 2–6)

To have a testimony of Jesus is to know that God the Father and Jesus Christ did indeed appear to the Prophet Joseph Smith to establish a new dispensation of His gospel so that salvation may be preached to all nations before He comes. . . .

To be valiant in a testimony of Jesus means that we accept . . . the prophetic mission of Joseph Smith and his successors and follow their counsel. ("Valiant in the Testimony of Jesus," *Tambuli,* June 1987, 2)

HOWARD W. HUNTER

Joseph Smith was not only a great man, but he was an inspired servant of the Lord, a prophet of God. His greatness consists in one thing—the truthfulness of his declaration that he saw the Father and the Son and that he responded to the reality of that divine revelation. . . .

I testify that the boy prophet, who in so many ways remains the central miracle in the 161 years of this church's experience, is living proof that, within God's hands and under the direction of the Savior of the world, weak and simple things should come forth and break down the mighty and strong ones. ("The Sixth Day of April, 1830," *Ensign,* May 1991, 63–64)

GORDON B. HINCKLEY

Great was the Prophet Joseph Smith's vision. It encompassed all the peoples of mankind, wherever they live, and all generations who have walked the earth and passed on. How can anyone, past or present, speak against him except out of ignorance? They have not tasted of his words; they have not pondered about him, nor prayed about him. As one who has done these things, I add my own words of testimony that he was and is a prophet of God, raised up as an instrument in the hands of the Almighty to usher in a new and final gospel dispensation. (*Teachings of Gordon B. Hinckley,* 1997, 503)

I bear solemn testimony of the divinity of his call, of the magnitude of his accomplishments, of the virtue of his life, and of the security of his place among the great and honored of the Almighty in all generations of time. (*Teachings of Gordon B. Hinckley,* 1997, 510)

I was not acquainted with the Prophet Joseph Smith, nor did I ever hear him speak. My grandfather, who as a young man lived in Nauvoo, did hear him and testified of his divine calling as the great prophet of this dispensation. But I feel I have come to know the Prophet Joseph Smith.

I have read and believed his testimony of his great first vision in which he conversed with the Father and the Son. I have pondered the wonder of that as I have stood in the grove where he prayed, and in that environment, by the power of the Spirit, I have received a witness that it happened as he said it happened.

I have read the Book of Mormon, which he translated by the gift and power of God. By the power of the Holy Ghost I have received a testimony and a witness of the divine origin of this sacred record. Joseph Smith did not write it of his own capacity.

I have seen with my own eyes the power of the priesthood which came to him under the hands of those who held it anciently. I have studied his life and measured his words. I have pondered the circumstances of his death, and I have come to know him—at least in some degree, at least enough that I can stand before you and testify that he was a prophet called and ordained to stand as God's instrument in this great work of restoration. ("'Believe His Prophets,'" *Ensign,* May 1992, 50–51)

How great indeed is our debt to [the Prophet Joseph Smith]. . . .

He was the instrument in the hands of the Almighty. He was the servant acting under the direction of the Lord Jesus Christ in bringing to pass this great latter-day work.

We stand in reverence before him. He is the great prophet of this dispensation. He stands at the head of this great and mighty work which is spreading across the earth. He is our prophet, our revelator, our seer, our friend. Let us not forget him. . . . God be thanked for the Prophet Joseph. (*Teachings of Gordon B. Hinckley,* 1997, 514)

WORDS OF THE
THE PROPHET

ACCOUNTABILITY

And I also beheld that all children who die before they arrive at the years of accountability, are saved in the celestial kingdom of heaven. (*HC* 2:381)

We believe that men will be punished for their own sins, and not for Adam's transgression. (A of F 1:2)

Each soul must be accountable to its Creator for its deed; and no person who has not reached the years of individual accountability is condemned for the non-performance of ceremonies or ordinances which he can neither understand nor attend to. Infants are all saved in Christ and need no penance, no baptism, no church membership. But a man who has heard the word of God is personally responsible for his own life and must bear the consequences of its rejection in his own person. (*The Life of Joseph Smith, the Prophet,* 78)

We believe that governments were instituted of God for the benefit of man; and that he holds men accountable for their acts in relation to them, both in making laws and administering them, for the good and safety of society. (D&C 134:1)

Men not unfrequently forget that they are dependent upon heaven for every blessing which they are permitted to enjoy, and that for every opportunity granted them they are to give an account. (*HC* 2:23–24)

After this instruction, you will be responsible for your own sins; it is a desirable honor that you should so walk before our heavenly Father as to save yourselves; we are all responsible to God for the manner we improve the light and wisdom given by our Lord to enable us to save ourselves. (*TPJS*, 234)

ADAM

Adam was created in the very fashion, image and likeness of God, and received instruction from, and walked, talked and conversed with Him, as one man talks and communes with another. (*HC* 6:305)

Adam did not commit sin in eating the fruits, for God had decreed that he should eat and fall. But in compliance with the decree, he should die. Only [that] he should die was the saying of the Lord; therefore the Lord appointed us to fall and also redeemed us. (*Commentary,* 14)

Adam holds the keys of the Dispensation of the Fulness of Times; i.e., the dispensation of all the times have been and will be revealed through him from the beginning to Christ, and from Christ to the end of all the dispensations that are to be revealed. (*Discourses,* 52–53)

The Father called all spirits before Him at the creation of man, and organized them. He (Adam) is the head, and was told to multiply. The keys were first given to him, and by him to others. He will have to give an account of his stewardship, and they to him. (*HC* 3:387)

Daniel in his seventh chapter speaks of the Ancient of Days; he means the oldest man, our Father Adam, Michael, he will call his children together and hold a council with them to prepare them for the coming of the Son of Man. He (Adam) is the father of the human family, and presides over the spirits of all men, and all that have had the keys must stand before him in this grand council. This may take place before some of us leave this stage of action. The Son of Man stands before him, and there is given him glory and dominion. Adam delivers up his stewardship to Christ, that which was delivered to him as holding the keys of the universe, but retains his standing as head of the human family. (*TPJS*, 160)

[God] set the ordinances to be the same forever and ever, and set Adam to watch over them, to reveal them from heaven to man, or to send angels to reveal them. "Are they not all ministering spirits, sent forth to minister for them who shall be heirs of salvation?" (Hebrews i, 14).

These angels are under the direction of Michael or Adam, who acts under the direction of the Lord. (*Encyclopedia*, 21)

[Adam was he] to whom Christ was first revealed, and through whom Christ has been revealed from heaven, and will continue to be revealed from henceforth. (*Encyclopedia*, 345)

I saw Adam in the valley of Adam-ondi-Ahman. He called together his children and blessed them with a patriarchal blessing. The Lord appeared in their midst, and he (Adam) blessed the all, and foretold what should befall them to the latest generation.

This is why Adam blessed his posterity; he wanted to bring them into the presence of God. (*HC* 3:338)

ADVERSITY

Profitable if not sweet are the uses of adversity. (*HC* 2:xxxii)

Never exact of a friend in adversity what you would require in prosperity.

If a man prove himself to be honest in his deal, and an enemy come upon him wickedly, through fraud or false pretences and because he is stronger than he, maketh him his prisoner and spoil him with his goods, never say unto that man in the day of his adversity, pay me what thou owest, for if thou doest it, thou addest a deeper wound, and condemnation shall come upon thee and thy riches shall be justified in the days of thine adversity if they mock at thee. (*TPJS*, 328)

Trials will only give us the knowledge necessary to understand the minds of the ancients. For my part, I think I never could have felt as I now do, if I had not suffered the wrongs that I have suffered. All things shall work together for good to them that love God. (*HC* 3:286)

The trials they have had to pass through shall work together for their good, and prepare them for the society of those who have come up out of great tribulation, and have washed their robes and made them white in the blood of the Lamb. (*HC* 3:330–31)

AGENCY

Resist evil, and there is no danger; God, men, and angels will not condemn those that resist everything that is evil, and devils cannot; as well might the devil seek to dethrone Jehovah, as overthrow an innocent soul that resists everything which is evil. (*HC* 4:605)

We do not wish by this to take your agency from you; but we feel to be plain, and pointed in our advice for we wish to do our duty, that your sins may not be found in our skirts. All persons are entitled to their agency, for God has so ordained it. He has constituted mankind moral agents, and given them power to choose good or evil; to seek after that which is good, by pursuing the pathway of holiness in this life, which brings peace of mind, and joy in the Holy Ghost here, and a fulness of joy and happiness at His right hand hereafter; or to pursue an evil course, going on in sin and rebellion against God, thereby bringing condemnation to their souls in this world, and an eternal loss in the world to come. (*HC* 4:45)

I do not govern them: I teach men correct principles, and they govern themselves. (*Joseph Smith, the Prophet-Teacher*, 65)

We deem it a just principle, and it is one the force of which we believe ought to be duly considered by every individual, that all men are created equal, and that all have the privilege of thinking for themselves upon all matters relative to conscience. Consequently, then, we are not disposed, had we the power, to deprive any one of exercising that free independence of mind which heaven has so graciously bestowed upon the human family as one of its choicest gifts. (*HC* 2:6–7)

It is one of the first principles of my life, and one that I have cultivated from my childhood, having been taught it by my father, to allow every one the liberty of conscience. (*HC* 6:56)

I have intended my remarks for all, both rich and poor, bond and free, great and small. I have no enmity against any man. I love you all; but I hate some of your deeds. I am your best friend, and if persons miss their mark it is their own fault. (*HC* 6:317)

ANGELS

Gods have an ascendancy over the angels, who are ministering servants. In the resurrection, some are raised to be angels; others are raised to become Gods. (*Discourses*, 43)

Men and angels are to be co-workers in bringing to pass this great work. (*Discourses*, 191)

We may look for angels and receive their ministrations, but we are to try the spirits and prove them, for it is often the case that men make a mistake in regard to these things. (*HC* 3:391)

An angel of God never has wings. Some will say that they have seen a spirit; that he offered them his hand, but they did not touch it. This is a lie. First, it is contrary to the plan of God: a spirit cannot come but in glory; an angel has flesh and bones; we see not their glory. The devil may appear as an angel of light. Ask God to reveal it; if it be of the devil, he will flee from you: if of God, He will manifest Himself, or make it manifest. (*HC* 3:392)

APOSTASY

I will give you one of the Keys of the mysteries of the Kingdom. It is an eternal principle, that has existed with God from all eternity: That man who rises up to condemn others, finding fault with the Church, saying that they are out of the way, while he himself is righteous, then know assuredly, that that man is in the high road to apostasy; and if he does not repent, will apostatize, as God lives. (*TPJS*, 159)

Strange as it may appear at first thought, yet it is no less so than true, that with all the professed determination to live godly, after turning from the faith of Christ, apostates have, unless they have speedily repented, sooner or later fallen into the snares of the wicked one and have been left destitute of the Spirit of God, to manifest their wickedness in the eyes of multitudes. (*Commentary*, 152)

Beware of all disaffected characters, for they come not to build up, but to destroy and scatter abroad. Though we or an angel from heaven preach any other gospel or introduce [any] order of things [other] than those things which ye have received and are authorized to receive from the First Presidency, let him be accursed. (*Commentary*, 173)

From apostates the faithful have received the severest persecutions. Judas was rebuked and immediately betrayed his Lord into the hands of His enemies, because Satan entered into him. There is a superior intelligence bestowed upon such as obeyed the Gospel with full purpose of heart, which, if sinned against, the apostate is left naked and destitute of the Spirit of God, and he is, in truth, nigh unto cursing, and his end is to be burned. When once that light which was in them is taken from them they become as much darkened as they were previously enlightened, and then, no marvel, if all their power should be enlisted against the truth, and they, Judas like, seek the destruction of those who were their greatest benefactors. What nearer friend on earth, or in heaven, had Judas than the Savior? (*HC* 2:23)

Christ said to His disciples (Mark 16:17 and 18), that these signs should follow them that believe:—"In my name shall they cast out devils; they shall speak with new tongues; they shall take up serpents; and if they drink any deadly thing it shall not hurt them; they shall lay hands on the sick, and they shall recover;" and also, in connection with this, read 1st Corinthians, 12th chapter. By the foregoing testimonies we may look at the Christian world and see the apostasy there has been from the apostolic platform. (*HC* 1:314)

I think that it is high time for a Christian world to awake out of sleep, and cry mightily to that God, day and night, whose anger we have justly incurred. Are not these things a sufficient stimulant to arouse the faculties, and call forth the energies of every man, woman or child, that possesses feelings of sympathy for their fellows, or that is in any degree endeared to the budding cause of our glorious Lord? I leave an intelligent community to answer this important question, with a confession, that this is what has caused me to overlook my own inability, and expose my weakness to a learned world; but, trusting in that God who has said that these things are hid from the wise and prudent and revealed unto babes, I step forth into the field to tell you what the Lord is doing, and what you must do, to enjoy the smiles of your Savior in these last days. (*TPJS*, 11)

ATONEMENT

We believe that through the atonement of Christ all mankind may be saved by obedience to the laws and ordinances of the Gospel. (A of F 1:3)

Whenever the Lord revealed Himself to men in ancient days, and commanded them to offer sacrifice to Him, . . . it was done that they might look forward in faith to the time of His coming, and rely upon the power of that atonement for a remission of their sins. And this they have done, thousands who have gone before us, whose garments are spotless, and who are, like Job, waiting with an assurance like his, that they will see Him in the *latter day* upon the earth, even in their flesh.

We may conclude, that though there were different dispensations, yet all things which God communicated to His people were calculated to draw their minds to the great object, and to teach them to rely upon God alone as the author of their salvation, as contained in His law. (*HC* 2:17)

I believe that God . . . foreordained the fall of man; but all merciful as he is, he foreordained at the same time, a plan of redemption of all mankind. I believe in the Divinity of Jesus Christ, and that He died for the sins of all men, who in Adam had fallen. (*HC* 4:78)

The fundamental principles of our religion are the testimony of the Apostles and Prophets, concerning Jesus Christ, that He died, was buried, and rose again the third day, and ascended into heaven; and all other things which pertain to our religion are only appendages to it. (*HC* 3:30)

The salvation of Jesus Christ was wrought out for all men, in order to triumph over the devil; for if it did not catch him in one place, it would in another; for he stood up as a Savior. All will suffer until they obey Christ himself. (*Discourses,* 223)

Through the atonement of Christ and the resurrection and obedience in the gospel, we shall again be conformed to the image of [God's] Son, Jesus Christ. Then we shall have attained to the image, glory, and character of God. (*Encyclopedia,* 56)

[Man] had departed from [God] and refused to be governed by those laws which God had given by His own voice from on high in the beginning. But notwithstanding the transgression, by which man had cut himself off from an immediate intercourse with his Maker without a Mediator, it appears that the great and glorious plan of His redemption was previously provided; the sacrifice prepared; the atonement wrought out in the mind and purpose of God, even in the person of the Son, through whom man was now to look for acceptance and through whose merits he was now taught that he alone could find redemption, since the word had been pronounced, Unto dust thou shalt return.

But that man was not able himself to erect a system, or plan with power sufficient to free him from a destruction which awaited him is evident from the fact that God, as before remarked, prepared a sacrifice in the gift of His own Son who should be sent in due time, to prepare a way, or open a door through which man might enter into the Lord's presence, whence he had been cast out for disobedience. From time to time these glad tidings were sounded in the ears of men in different ages of the world down to the time of Messiah's coming. (*HC* 2:15)

BAPTISM

You might as well baptize a bag of sand as a man, if not done in view of the remission of sins and getting of the Holy Ghost. Baptism by water is but half a baptism, and is good for nothing without the other half—that is, the baptism of the Holy Ghost. (*HC* 5:499)

Baptism is a holy ordinance preparatory to the reception of the Holy Ghost; it is the channel and key by which the Holy Ghost will be administered. (*HC* 3:379)

Baptism is a covenant with God that we will do his will. (*Discourses,* 273)

There is one God, one Father, one Jesus, on hope of our calling, one baptism. * * * Many talk of baptism not being essential to salvation; but this kind of teaching would lay the foundation of their damnation. I have the truth, and am at the defiance of the world to contradict me, if they can. (*TPJS,* 374)

Many objections are urged against the Latter-day Saints for not admitting the validity of sectarian baptism, and for withholding fellowship from sectarian churches. Yet to do otherwise would be like putting new wine into old bottles, and putting old wine into new bottles. (*TPJS,* 197)

I contend that baptism is a sign ordained of God, for the believer in Christ to take upon himself in order to enter into the kingdom of God, "for except ye are born of water and of the Spirit ye cannot enter into the Kingdom of God," said the Savior. It is a sign and a commandment which God has set for man to enter into His kingdom.

Those who seek to enter in any other way will seek in vain; for God will not receive them, neither will the angels acknowledge their works as accepted, for they have not obeyed the ordinances, nor attended to the signs which God ordained for the salvation of man, to prepare him for, and give him a title to, a celestial glory; and God had decreed that all who will not obey His voice shall not escape the damnation of hell. What is the damnation of hell? To go with that society who have not obeyed His commands. (TPJS, 203)

Upon looking over the sacred pages of the Bible, searching into the prophets and sayings of the apostles, we find no subject so nearly connected with salvation, as that of baptism. In the first place, however, let us understand that the word baptize is derived from the Greek verb "baptiso," and means to immerse or overwhelm, and that sprinkle is from the Greek verb "rantiso," and means to scatter on by particles; then we can treat the subject as one inseparably connected with our eternal welfare; and always bear in mind that it is one of the only methods by which we can obtain a remission of sins in this world, and be prepared to enter into the joys of our Lord in the world to come. (*Discourses*, 92–93)

All children are redeemed by the blood of Jesus Christ, and the moment they leave this world they are taken to the bosom of Abraham. (*Discourses,* 273)

In the former ages of the world, before the Savior came in the flesh, "the saints" were baptized in the name of Jesus Christ to come, because there never was any other name whereby men could be saved; and after he came in the flesh and was crucified, then the saints were baptized in the name of Jesus Christ, crucified, risen from the dead and ascended into heaven, that they might be buried in baptism like him, and be raised in glory like him, that as there was but one Lord, one faith, one baptism, and one God and father of us all, even so there was but one door to the mansions of bliss. (*Encyclopedia,* 66–67)

BAPTISM FOR THE DEAD

The Bible supports the doctrine [of baptism for the dead]. If there is one word of the Lord that supports the doctrine, it is enough to make it a true doctrine. Again, if we can baptize a man in the name of the Father, [and] of the Son, and of the Holy Ghost for the remission of sins, it is just as much our privilege to act as an agent and be baptized for the remission of sins for and in behalf of our dead kindred who have not heard the gospel or fulness of it. (*Commentary*, 170)

And now as the great purposes of God are hastening to their accomplishment and the things spoken of in the prophets are fulfilling, as the kingdom of God is established on the earth, and the ancient order of things restored, the Lord has manifested to us this day and privilege, and we are commanded to be baptized for our dead, thus fulfilling the words of Obadiah, when speaking of the glory of the latter-day: "And saviours shall come up on mount Zion to judge the remnant of Esau, and the kingdom shall be the Lord's." (*Encyclopedia*, 70)

Ordinances instituted in the heavens before the foundation of the world, in the priesthood, for the salvation of men, are not to be altered or changed. All must be saved on the same principles.

It is for the same purpose that God gathers together His people in the last days, to build unto the Lord a house to prepare them for the ordinances and endowments, washings and anointings, etc. One of the ordinances of the house of the Lord is baptism for the dead. God decreed before the foundation of the world that

that ordinance should be administered in a font prepared for that purpose in the house of the Lord. (*HC* 5:423–24)

This doctrine presents in a clear light the wisdom and mercy of God in preparing an ordinance for the salvation of the dead, being baptized by proxy, their names recorded in heaven and they judged according to the deeds done in the body. This doctrine was the burden of the scriptures. Those Saints who neglect it in behalf of their deceased relatives, do it at the peril of their own salvation. (*TPJS,* 197)

BIBLE

From sundry revelations which had been received, it was apparent that many important points touching the salvation of men, had been taken from the Bible, or lost before it was compiled. (*TPJS,* 6–7)

He that can mark the power of Omnipotence, inscribed upon the heavens, can also see God's own handwriting in the sacred volume [of the Bible]: and he who reads it oftenest will like it best, and he who is acquainted with it, will know the hand wherever he can see it; and when once discovered, it will not only receive an acknowledgment, but an obedience to all his heavenly precepts. (*HC* 2:14)

We believe the Bible to be the word of God as far as it is translated correctly. (A of F 1:8)

First—"Do you believe the Bible?"

If we do, we are the only people under heaven that does, for there are none of the religious sects of the day that do.

Second—"Wherein do you differ from other sects?"

In that we believe the Bible, and all other sects profess to believe their interpretations of the Bible, and their creeds. (*HC* 3:28)

We have not found the Book of Jasher, nor any other of the lost books mentioned in the Bible as yet; nor will we obtain them at present. Respecting the Apocrypha, the Lord said to us that there were many things in it which were true, and there were many things in it which were not true, and to those who desire it, should be given by the Spirit to know the true from the false. (*HC* 1:363)

BOOK OF MORMON

I told the brethren that the Book of Mormon was the most correct of any book on earth, and the keystone of our religion, and a man would get nearer to God by abiding by its precepts, than by any other book. (*HC* 4:461)

Take away the Book of Mormon and the revelations, and where is our religion? We have none. (*HC* 2:52)

The Book of Mormon is true, just what it purports to be, and for this testimony I expect to give an account in the day of judgment. (*Encyclopedia,* 86–87)

I did translate the Book of Mormon by the gift and power of God, and it is before the world; and all the powers of earth and hell cannot rob me of it. (*Encyclopedia,* 92)

Let us take the Book of Mormon, which a man took and hid in his field, securing it by his faith, to spring up in the last days, or in due time; let us behold it coming forth out of the ground, which is indeed accounted the least of all seeds, but behold it branching forth, yea, even towering, with lofty branches, and God-like majesty, until it, like the mustard seed, becomes the greatest of all herbs. And it is truth, and it has sprouted and come forth out of the earth, and righteousness begins to look down from heaven, and God is sending down his powers, gifts and angels, to lodge in the branches thereof. (*Discourses,* 258–59)

CALLING AND ELECTION

The other Comforter spoken of is a subject of great interest, and perhaps understood by few of this generation. After a person has faith in Christ, repents of his sins, and is baptized for the remission of his sins and receives the Holy Ghost, (by the laying on of hands), which is the first Comforter, then let him continue to humble himself before God, hungering and thirsting after righteousness, and living by every word of God, and the Lord will soon say unto him, Son, thou shalt be exalted. When the Lord has thoroughly proved him, and finds that the man is determined to serve him at all hazards, then the man will find his calling and his election made sure, then it will be his privilege to receive the other Comforter, which the Lord hath promised the Saints, as is recorded in the testimony of St. John, in the 14th chapter, from the 14th to the 27th verses. (*Discourses,* 41–42)

Contend earnestly for the like precious faith with the Apostle Peter, "and add to your faith virtue," knowledge, temperance, patience, godliness, brotherly kindness, charity; "for if these things be in you, and abound, they make you that ye shall neither be barren nor unfruitful in the knowledge of our Lord Jesus Christ." Another point, after having all these qualifications, he lays this injunction upon the people "to make your calling and election sure." He is emphatic upon this subject— after adding all this virtue, knowledge, &c., "Make your calling and election sure." . . .

We have no claim in our eternal compact, in relation to eternal things, unless our actions and contracts and all things tend to this end. But after all this, you have got to make your calling and election sure. If this injunction would lie largely on those to whom it was spoken, how much more those of the present generation! (*HC* 5:402–3)

Now for the secret and grand key. Though they might hear the voice of God and know that Jesus was the Son of God, this would be no evidence that their election and calling was made sure, that they had part with Christ, and were joint heirs with Him. They then would want that more sure word of prophecy, that they were sealed in the heavens and had the promise of eternal life in the kingdom of God. Then, having this promise sealed unto them, it was an anchor to the soul, sure and steadfast. Though the thunders might roll and lightnings flash, and earthquakes bellow, and war gather thick around, yet this hope and knowledge would support the soul in every hour of trial, trouble and tribulation. Then knowledge through our Lord and Savior Jesus Christ is the grand key that unlocks the glories and mysteries of the kingdom of heaven. . . . Then I would exhort you to go on and continue to call upon God until you make your calling and election sure for yourselves, by obtaining this more sure word of prophecy, and wait patiently for the promise until you obtain it, &c. (*HC* 5:388–89)

CELESTIAL KINGDOM

And again we bear record—for we saw and heard, and this is the testimony of the gospel of Christ concerning them who shall come forth in the resurrection of the just—

They are they who received the testimony of Jesus, and believed on his name and were baptized after the manner of his burial, being buried in the water in his name, and this according to the commandment which he has given . . .

And who overcome by faith, and are sealed by the Holy Spirit of promise, which the Father sheds forth upon all those who are just and true. . . .

These shall dwell in the presence of God and his Christ forever and ever. . . .

These are they who are come unto Mount Zion, and unto the city of the living God, the heavenly place, the holiest of all. . . .

These are they whose names are written in heaven, where God and Christ are the judge of all.

These are they who are just men made perfect through Jesus the mediator of the new covenant, who wrought out this perfect atonement through the shedding of his own blood.

These are they whose bodies are celestial, whose glory is that of the sun, even the glory of God, the highest of all, whose glory the sun of the firmament is written of as being typical. (D&C 76:50–51, 53, 62, 66, 68–70)

The heavens were opened upon us, and I beheld the celestial kingdom of God, and the glory thereof. . . .

I saw the transcendent beauty of the gate through which the heirs of that kingdom will enter; . . .

Also the blazing throne of God, whereon was seated the Father and the Son. . . . I saw Father Adam and Abraham; and my father and my mother; my brother Alvin, that has long since slept;

And marveled how it was that he had obtained an inheritance in that kingdom, seeing that he had departed this life before the Lord had set his hand to gather Israel the second time, and had not been baptized for the remission of sins.

Thus came the voice of the Lord unto me, saying: All who have died without a knowledge of this gospel, who would have received it if they had been permitted to tarry, shall be heirs of the celestial kingdom of God;

Also all that shall die henceforth without a knowledge of it, who would have received it with all their hearts, shall be heirs of that kingdom;

For I, the Lord, will judge all men according to their works, according to the desire of their hearts. (D&C 137:1–3, 5–9)

No one can ever enter the celestial kingdom unless he is strictly honest. (*Joseph Smith the Prophet,* 104)

I will proceed to tell you what the Lord requires of all people, high and low, rich and poor, male and female, ministers and people, professors of religion and non-professors, in order that they may enjoy the Holy Spirit of God to a fulness and escape the judgments of God, which are almost ready to burst upon the nations of the earth. Repent of all your sins, and be baptized in water for the remission of them, in the name of the Father, and of the Son, and of the Holy Ghost, and receive the ordinance of the laying on of the hands of him who is ordained and sealed unto this power, that ye may receive the Holy Spirit of God; and this is according to the Holy Scriptures, and the Book of Mormon; and the only way that man can enter into the celestial kingdom. (*HC* 1:314–15)

CELESTIAL MARRIAGE

In the celestial glory there are three heavens or degrees;

And in order to obtain the highest, a man must enter into this order of the priesthood [meaning the new and everlasting covenant of marriage];

And if he does not, he cannot obtain it.

He may enter into the other, but that is the end of his kingdom; he cannot have an increase. (D&C 131:1–4)

Except a man and his wife enter into an everlasting covenant and be married for eternity, while in this probation, by the power and authority of the Holy Priesthood, they will cease to increase when they die; that is, they will not have any children after the resurrection. But those who are married by the power and authority of the priesthood in this life, and continue without committing the sin against the Holy Ghost, will continue to increase and have children in the celestial glory. (*HC* 5:391)

I . . . touched upon the subject of the everlasting covenant, showing that a man and his wife must enter into that covenant in the world, or he will have no claim on her in the next world. (*HC* 5:510)

CHARITY

It comes to show that all men's religion is vain without charity. (*HC* 1:275)

I then addressed them and gave much instruction calculated to guard them against self-sufficiency, self-righteousness, and self-importance; touching upon many subjects of importance and value to all who wish to walk humbly before the Lord, and especially teaching them to observe charity, wisdom and fellow-feeling, with love one towards another in all things, and under all circumstances. (*HC* 3:383)

If honor dignifies an honest people, if virtue exalts a community, if wisdom guides great men, if principle governs intelligent beings, if humanity spreads comfort among the needy, and if religion affords consolation by showing that charity is the first, best and sweetest token of perfect love, then . . . search diligently till you find [it]. (*HC* 6:247)

I do not dwell upon your faults, and you shall not upon mine. Charity, which is love, covereth a multitude of sins, and I have often covered up all the faults among you; but the prettiest thing is to have no faults at all. We should cultivate a meek, quiet and peaceable spirit. (*HC* 5:517)

My heart is large enough for all men. (*HC* 6:459)

Until we have perfect love we are liable to fall and when we have a testimony that our names are sealed in the Lamb's book of life we have perfect love and then it is impossible for false Christs to deceive us. (*TPJS*, 5–6)

Love is one of the chief characteristics of Deity, and ought to be manifested by those who aspire to be the sons of God. A man filled with the love of God, is not content with blessing his family alone, but ranges through the whole world, anxious to bless the whole human race. (*TPJS*, 178)

In order to conduct the affairs of the Kingdom in righteousness, it is all important that the most perfect harmony, kind feeling, good understanding, and confidence should exist in the hearts of all the brethren; and that true charity, love one towards another, should characterize all their proceedings. If there are any uncharitable feelings, any lack of confidence, then pride, arrogance and envy will soon be manifested; confusion must inevitably prevail, and the authorities of the Church set at naught. (*HC* 4:165)

CHASTENING

Because we will not receive chastisement at the hand of the Prophet and Apostles, the Lord chastiseth us with sickness and death. Let not any man publish his own righteousness, for others can see that for him; sooner let him confess his sins, and then he will be forgiven, and he will bring forth more fruit. When a corrupt man is chastised he gets angry and will not endure it. (*HC* 4:478–79)

We have been chastened by the hand of God heretofore for not obeying His commands, although we never violated any human law, or transgressed any human precept; yet we have treated lightly His commands, and departed from His ordinances, and the Lord has chastened us sore, and we have felt His arm and kissed the rod; let us be wise in time to come and ever remember that "to obey is better than sacrifice, and to hearken than the fat of rams." (*HC* 5:65)

I frequently rebuke and admonish my brethren, and that because I love them, not because I wish to incur their displeasure, or mar their happiness. Such a course of conduct is not calculated to gain the good will of all, but rather the ill will of many; therefore, the situation in which I stand is an important one; so, you see, brethren, the higher the authority, the greater the difficulty of the station; but these rebukes and admonitions become necessary, from the perverseness of the brethren, for their temporal as well as spiritual welfare. They actually constitute a part of the duties of my station and calling. (*HC* 2:478)

The scourge must come; repentance and humility may mitigate the chastisement, but cannot altogether avert it. (*HC* 2:107)

COMMANDMENTS

We cannot keep all the commandments without first knowing them, and we cannot expect to know all, or more than we now know unless we comply with or keep those we have already received. (*HC* 5:135)

Be virtuous and pure; be men of integrity and truth; keep the commandments of God; and then you will be able more perfectly to understand the difference between right and wrong—between the things of God and the things of men; and your path will be like that of the just, which shineth brighter and brighter unto the perfect day. (*TPJS*, 254)

You, who do the will of the Lord and keep His commandments, have need to rejoice with unspeakable joy, for such shall be exalted very high, and shall be lifted up in triumph above all the kingdoms of this world. (*HC* 1:299)

And gave unto them commandments that they should love and serve him, the only living and true God, and that he should be the only being whom they should worship. (D&C 20:19.)

That by keeping the commandments they might be washed and cleansed from all their sins, and receive the Holy Spirit by the laying on of the hands of him who is ordained and sealed unto this power. (D&C 76:52.)

COMPASSION

The nearer we get to our heavenly Father, the more we are disposed to look with compassion on perishing souls; we feel that we want to take them upon our shoulders, and cast their sins behind our backs. . . . If you would have God have mercy on you, have mercy on one another. (*HC* 5:24)

This doctrine [redeeming the dead] appears glorious, inasmuch as it exhibits the greatness of divine compassion and benevolence in the extent of the plan of human salvation. This glorious truth is well calculated to enlarge the understanding, and to sustain the soul under troubles, difficulties, and distresses. (*The Words of Joseph Smith*, 77–78)

God does not look on sin with allowance, but when men have sinned, there must be allowance made for them. . . . The nearer we get to our heavenly Father, the more are we disposed to look with compassion on perishing souls; we feel that we want to take them upon our shoulders, and cast their sins behind our backs. (*HC* 5:24)

CONTENTION

It has been our study to avoid contention, and we have never interfered with others until they have thrown down the gauntlet; and as we have not been up to the present the aggressors so we are determined for the future not to be the aggressors. (*HC* 5:381)

COVENANTS

And we would say to all the Saints who have made a covenant with the Lord by sacrifice, that, inasmuch as you are faithful, you shall not lose your reward. (*HC* 3:394)

And may God enable us to perform our vows and covenants with each other, in all fidelity and righteousness before Him, that our influence may be felt among the nations of the earth, in mighty power, even to rend the kingdoms of darkness asunder, and triumph over priestcraft and spiritual wickedness in high places, and break in pieces all kingdoms that are opposed to the kingdom of Christ, and spread the light and truth of the everlasting Gospel from the rivers to the ends of the earth. (*HC* 2:375)

I despise a hypocrite or a covenant breaker (*Encyclopedia,* 150)

Our covenants here are of no force one with another except made in view of eternity. (*Encyclopedia,* 151)

It requires two parties to make a covenant, and those two parties must be agreed or no covenant can be made. (*Commentary,* 56)

Covenants, either there or here, must be made in view of eternity. And the covenant sealed on the foreheads of the parents secures the children from falling, that they shall all sit upon thrones as one with the Godhead, joint heirs of God with Jesus Christ. This principle is revealed also through the covenant of Abraham and his children. (*Commentary,* 224)

COVETOUSNESS

Be admonished, then, O ye Saints! And let not covetousness, which is idolatry, nor worldly ambition hinder you. (*HC* 2:517)

DEATH

These are the first principles of consolation. How consoling to the mourners when they are called to part with a husband, wife, father, mother, child, or dear relative, to know that, although the earthly tabernacle is laid down and dissolved, they shall rise again to dwell . . . in immortal glory, not to sorrow, suffer, or die any more, but they shall be heirs of God and joint heirs with Jesus Christ. (*HC* 6:306)

What have we to console us in relation to the dead? We have reason to have the greatest hope and consolation for our dead of any people on the earth; for we have seen them walk worthily in our midst, and seen them sink asleep in the arms of Jesus; and those who have died in the faith are now in the celestial kingdom of God. And hence is the glory of the sun. (*HC* 6:315)

With respect to the deaths in Zion, we feel to mourn with those that mourn, but remember that the God of all the earth will do right. (*HC* 1:341)

It mattereth not whether we live long or short on the earth after we come to a knowledge of these principles [of the gospel] and obey them unto the end. (*HC* 4:555)

The Lord takes many away even in infancy, that they may escape the envy of man, and the sorrows and evils of this present world; they were too pure, too lovely, to live on earth; therefore, if rightly considered, instead of mourning we have reason to rejoice as they are delivered from evil, and we shall soon have them again. (*TPJS*, 201–202)

The only difference between the old and young dying is, one lives longer in heaven and eternal light and glory than the other, and is freed a little sooner from this miserable wicked world. Notwithstanding all this glory, we for a moment lose sight of it, and mourn the loss, but we do not mourn as those without hope. (*TPJS*, 202)

More painful to me are the thoughts of annihilation than death. If I have no expectation of seeing my father, mother, brothers, sisters and friends again, my heart would burst in a moment, and I should go down to my grave. (*Encyclopedia*, 160)

All men know that they must die. And it is important that we should understand the reasons and causes of our exposure to the vicissitudes of life and of death, and the designs and purposes of God in our coming into the world, our sufferings here, and our departure hence. What is the object of our coming into existence, then dying and falling away, to be here no more? It is but reasonable to suppose that God would reveal something in reference to the matter, and it is a subject we ought to study more than any other. We ought to study it day and night, for the world is ignorant in reference to their true condition and relation. If we have any claim on our Heavenly Father for anything, it is for knowledge on this important subject. Could we read and comprehend all that has been written from the days of Adam, on the relation of man to God and angels in a future state, we should know very little about it. Reading the experience of others, or the revelation given to *them*, can never give *us* a comprehensive view of our condition and true relation to God. Knowledge of these things can only be obtained by experience through the ordinances of God set forth for that purpose. (*HC* 6:50)

DEGREES OF GLORY

Nothing could be more pleasing to the Saints upon the order of the kingdom of the Lord, than the light which burst upon the world through the foregoing vision [D&C 76]. Every law, every commandment, every promise, every truth, and every point touching the destiny of man, from Genesis to Revelation, where the purity of the scriptures remains unsullied by the folly of men, go to show the perfection of the theory [of different degrees of glory in the future life] and witnesses the fact that that document is a transcript from the records of the eternal world. The sublimity of the ideas; the purity of the language; the scope for action; the continued duration for completion, in order that the heirs of salvation may confess the Lord and bow the knee; the rewards for faithfulness, and the punishments for sins, are so much beyond the narrow-mindedness of men, that every honest man is constrained to explain: "It came from God." (*HC* 1:252–53)

Go and read the vision in the Book of Covenants [section 76]. There is clearly illustrated glory upon glory—one glory of the sun, another glory of the moon, and a glory of the stars; and as one star differeth from another star in glory, even so do they of the telestial world differ in glory, and every man who reigns in celestial glory is a God to his dominions. (*HC* 6:477)

I do not believe the . . . doctrine of sending honest men and noble-minded men to hell, along with the murderer and the adulterer. They may hurl all their hell and fiery billows upon me, for they will roll off me as fast as they come on. But I have an order of things to save the poor fellows at any rate, and get them saved; for I will send men to preach to them in prison and save them if I can.

There are mansions for those who obey a celestial law, and there are other mansions for those who come short of the law, every man in his own order. (*HC* 6:365)

The great misery of departed spirits in the world of spirits, where they go after death, is to know that they come short of the glory that others enjoy and that they might have enjoyed themselves, and they are their own accusers. "But," says one, "I believe in one universal heaven and hell, where all go, and are all alike, and equally miserable or equally happy."

What! where all are huddled together—the honorable, virtuous, and murderers, and whoremongers, when it is written that they shall be judged according to the deeds done in the body? But St. Paul informs us of three glories and three heavens. He knew a man that was caught up to the third heavens. Now, if the doctrine of the sectarian world, that there is but one heaven, is true, Paul, what do you tell that lie for, and say there are three? Jesus said unto His disciples, "In my Father's house are many mansions, if it were not so, I would have told you. I go to prepare a place for you, and I will come and receive you to myself, that where I am ye may be also." (*TPJS*, 321)

I could explain a hundred fold more than I ever have of the glories of the kingdoms manifested to me in the vision, were I permitted, and were the people prepared to receive them. (*HC* 5:402)

DEVIL

All beings who have bodies have power over those who have not. The devil has no power over us only as we permit him. The moment we revolt at anything which comes from God, the devil takes power. (*Discourses,* 82)

The devil can speak in tongues; the adversary will come with his work; he can tempt all classes. (*HC* 3:392)

I have learned by experience that the enemy of truth does not slumber, nor cease his exertions to bias the minds of communities against the servants of the Lord, by stirring up the indignation of men upon all matters of importance or interest. (*HC* 2:437)

He . . . observed that Satan was generally blamed for the evils which we did, but if he was the cause of all our wickedness, men could not be condemned. The devil could not compel mankind to do evil; all was voluntary. Those who resisted the Spirit of God, would be liable to be led into temptation, and then the association of heaven would be withdrawn from those who refused to be made partakers of such great glory. God would not exert any compulsory means, and the devil could not; and such ideas as were entertained [on these subjects] by many were absurd. (*HC* 4:358)

The devil has great power to deceive; he will so transform things as to make one gape at those who are doing the will of God. (*HC* 4:605)

The punishment of the devil was that he should not have a habitation like men. The devil's retaliation is, he comes into this world, binds up men's bodies, and occupies them himself. When the authorities come along, they eject him from a stolen habitation. (*HC* 5:403)

DILIGENCE

Be faithful, be diligent, contend earnestly for the faith once delivered to the Saints; let every man, woman and child realize the importance of the work, and act as if success depended on his individual exertion alone; let all feel an interest in it. (*HC* 4:214)

EDUCATION

If children are to be brought up in the way they should go, to be good citizens here and happy hereafter, they must be taught. It is idle to suppose that children will grow up good, while surrounded with wickedness, without cultivation. It is folly to suppose that they can become learned without education. (*Discourses,* 273)

It is impossible for a man to be saved in ignorance. (*HC* 5:392)

But I beg leave to say unto you, brethren, that ignorance, superstition and bigotry placing itself where it ought not, is oftentimes in the way of the prosperity of this Church. (*TPJS*, 140)

All the minds and spirits that God ever sent into the world are susceptible of enlargement. (*Discourses*, 46)

I am a rough stone. The sound of the hammer and chisel was never heard on me until the Lord took me in hand. I desire the learning and wisdom of heaven alone. (*HC* 5:423)

We consider that God has created man with a mind capable of instruction, and a faculty which may be enlarged in proportion to the heed and diligence given to the light communicated from heaven to the intellect. (*HC* 2:8)

ENDOWMENT

In regard to the law of the Priesthood, there should be a place where all nations shall come up from time to time to receive their endowments. (*TPJS*, 380)

The endowment you are so anxious to hear about, you cannot comprehend now, nor could Gabriel explain it to the understanding of your minds; but strive to be prepared in your hearts, be faithful in all things, that when we meet in solemn assembly . . . be clean every whit. . . . If we are faithful, and live by every word that proceeds forth from the mouth of God, I will venture to prophesy that we shall get a blessing that will be worth remembering, if we should live as long as John the Revelator; our blessing will be such as we have not realized before . . . . The order of the house of God has been, and ever will be, the same, even after Christ comes; and after the termination of the thousand years it will be the same; and we shall finally enter into the celestial Kingdom of God, and enjoy it forever. (*Encyclopedia*, 215)

You need an endowment, brethren, in order that you may be prepared and able to overcome all things; and those that reject your testimony will be damned. The sick will be healed, the lame made to walk, the deaf to hear, and the blind to see, through your instrumentality. . . . But when you are endowed and prepared to preach the Gospel to all nations, kindreds, and tongues, in their own languages, you must faithfully warn all, and bind up the testimony, and seal up the law, and the destroying angel will follow close at your heels, and exercise his tremendous mission upon the children of disobedience; and destroy the workers of iniquity, while the Saints will be gathered out from among them, and stand in holy places ready to meet the Bridegroom when he comes. (*TPJS*, 2002, 90–91)

The endowment was to prepare the disciples for their missions unto the world. (*HC* 5:259)

ETERNAL LIFE

The scriptures inform us that "This is life eternal that they might know thee, the only true God, and Jesus Christ whom thou hast sent."

If any man does not know God, and inquires what kind of a being He is,—if he will search diligently his own heart—if the declaration of Jesus and the apostles be true, he will realize that he has not eternal life; for there can be eternal life on no other principle. (*HC* 6:304)

Here, then, is eternal life—to know the only wise and true God; and you have got to learn how to be gods yourselves, and to be kings and priests to God, the same as all gods have done before you, namely, by going from one small degree to another, and from a small capacity to a great one; from grace to grace, from exaltation to exaltation, until you attain to the resurrection of the dead, and are able to dwell in everlasting burnings, and to sit in glory, as do those who sit enthroned in everlasting power. And I want you to know that God, in the last days, while certain individuals are proclaiming His name, is not trifling with you or me. (*HC* 6:306)

Without the idea of the existence of the attributes which belong to God the minds of men could not have power to exercise faith in him so as to lay hold upon eternal life. (*Encyclopedia*, 1997, 233)

EXALTATION

When you climb up a ladder, you must begin at the bottom, and ascend step by step, until you arrive at the top; and so it is with the principles of the gospel—you must begin with the first, and go on until you learn all the principles of exaltation. But it will be a great while after you have passed through the veil before you will have learned them. It is not all to be comprehended in this world; it will be a great work to learn our salvation and exaltation even beyond the grave. (*HC* 6:306–7)

Truth, virtue, and honor, combined with energy and industry, pave the way to exaltation, glory and bliss. (*HC* 6:425)

If you wish to go where God is, you must be like God, or possess the principles which God possesses, for if we are not drawing towards God in principle, we are going away from Him and drawing towards the devil. (*HC* 4:588)

Let your heart be comforted; live in strict obedience to the commandments of God, and walk humbly before Him, and He will exalt thee in His own due time. (*HC* 1:408)

God brings low before He exalts. (*HC* 1:216)

FAITH

As many as would believe and be baptized in [Christ's] holy name, and endure in faith to the end, should be saved. (D&C 20:25.)

This is the testimony of the gospel of Christ concerning them who shall come forth in resurrection of the just—

They are they who received the testimony of Jesus, and believed on his name . . .

And who overcome by faith, and are sealed by the Holy Spirit of promise, which the Father sheds forth upon all those who are just and true. (D&C 76:50–51, 53)

It is . . . necessary, in order to the exercise of faith in God unto life and salvation, that men should have the idea of the existence of the attribute justice in him; for without the idea of the existence of the attribute justice in the Deity men could not have confidence sufficient to place themselves under his guidance and direction; for they would be filled with fear and doubt lest the judge of all the earth would not do right, and thus fear or doubt, existing in the mind, would preclude the possibility of the exercise of faith in him for life and salvation. . . .

And again, it is equally important that men should have the idea of the existence of the attribute mercy in the Deity, in order to exercise faith in him for life and salvation; for without the idea of the existence of this attribute in the Deity, the spirits of the saints would faint in the midst of the tribulations, afflictions, and persecutions which they have to endure for righteousness' sake. . . .

And lastly, but not less important to the exercise of faith in God, is the idea of the existence of the attribute truth in him; for without the idea of the existence of this attribute the mind of man could have nothing upon which it could rest with certainty—all would be confusion and doubt. . . .

In view, then, of the existence of these attributes, the faith of the saints can become exceedingly strong, abounding in righteousness unto the praise and glory of God, and can exert its mighty influence in searching after wisdom and understanding, until it has obtained a knowledge of all things that pertain to life and salvation. (*Lectures* 4:13,15–16, 18)

An actual knowledge to any person, that the course of life which he pursues is according to the will of God, is essentially necessary to enable him to have that confidence in God without which no person can obtain eternal life. (*Lectures* 6:2)

When a man works by faith he works by mental exertion instead of physical force. (*Lectures* 7:3)

Salvation is the effect of faith. (*Lectures* 7:17)

It was by obtaining a knowledge of God that men got the knowledge of all things which pertain to life and godliness, and this knowledge was the effect of faith; so that all things which pertain to life and godliness are the effects of faith. (*Lectures* 7:19)

When faith comes it brings its train of attendants with it—apostles, prophets, evangelists, pastors, teachers, gifts, wisdom, knowledge, miracles, healings, tongues, interpretation of tongues, etc. All these appear when faith appears on the earth, and disappear when it disappears from the earth; for these are the effects of faith, and always have attended, and always will, attend it. (*Lectures* 7:3)

What God may do for us I do not know, but I hope for the best always in all circumstances. Although I go unto death, I will trust in God. (*Writings,* 362; standardized)

Faith comes by hearing the word of God, through the testimony of the servants of God; that testimony is always attended by the Spirit of prophecy and revelation. . . .

Faith comes not by signs, but by hearing the word of God. (*HC* 3:379)

Because faith is wanting, the fruits are. No man since the world was had faith without having something along with it. The ancients quenched the violence of fire, escaped the edge of the sword, women received their dead, &c. By faith the worlds were made. A man who has none of the gifts has no faith; and he deceives himself, if he supposes he has. Faith has been wanting, not only among the heathen, but in professed Christendom also, so that tongues, healings, prophecy, and prophets and apostles, and all the gifts and blessings have been wanting. (*HC* 5:218)

If you have any darkness, you have only to ask, and the darkness is removed. It is not necessary that miracles should be wrought to remove darkness. Miracles are the fruits of faith.

"How then shall they call on Him in whom they have not believed? And how shall they hear without a preacher? And how shall they preach except they be sent?"

God may translate the scriptures by me if He chooses. Faith comes by hearing the word of God. If a man has not faith enough to do one thing, he may have faith to do another: if he cannot remove a mountain, he may heal the sick. Where faith is there will be some of the fruits: all gifts and power which were sent from heaven, were poured out on the heads of those who had faith. (*HC* 5:355)

FASTING

If the Saints are sick, or have sickness in their families, and the Elders do not prevail, every family should get power by fasting & prayer & anointing with oil & continue so to do, their sick shall be healed. (*The Words of Joseph Smith,* 37)

If we would be sober and watch in fasting and prayer, God would turn away sickness from our midst. (*HC* 6:52)

FOREORDINATION

Every man who has a calling to minister to the inhabitants of the world was ordained to that very purpose in the Grand Council of heaven before this world was. I suppose that I was ordained to this very office in that Grand Council. (*HC* 6:364)

I believe . . . that there is a God, possessing all the attributes ascribed to him by all Christians of all denominations; that he reigns over all things in heaven and on earth, and that all are subject to his power. . . . I believe that God foreknew everything, but did not foreordain everything; I deny that foreordain and foreknow is the same thing. He foreordained the fall of man; but all merciful as he is, he foreordained at the same time, a plan of redemption of all mankind. I believe in the Divinity of Jesus Christ, and that He died for the sins of all men, who in Adam had fallen. . . . I believe . . . that a man is a moral, responsible, free agent; that although it was foreordained he should fall, and be redeemed, yet after the redemption it was not foreordained that he should again sin. (*Discourses,* 11–12)

FORGIVENESS

Ever keep in exercise the principle of mercy, and be ready to forgive our brother on the first intimations of repentance, and asking forgiveness; and should we even forgive our brother, or even our enemy, before he repent or ask forgiveness, our Heavenly Father would be equally as merciful unto us. (*HC* 3:383)

I freely forgive all men. If we would secure and cultivate the love of others, we must love others, even our enemies as well as friends. (*HC* 5:498)

And the spirit of confession and forgiveness was mutual among us all, and we covenanted with each other, in the sight of God, and the holy angels, and the brethren, to strive thenceforward to build each other up in righteousness in all things, and not listen to evil reports concerning each other; but, like brothers indeed, go to each other, with our grievances, in the spirit of meekness, and be reconciled,

and thereby promote our happiness, and the happiness of the family, and, in short, the happiness
and well-being of all. (*HC* 2:353)

Thus you see, my dear brother, the willingness of
our heavenly Father to forgive sins, and restore to
favor all those who are willing to humble themselves before Him, and confess their sins, and forsake them, and return to Him with full purpose
of heart, acting no hypocrisy, to serve Him to the
end. (*HC* 2:315)

One of the most pleasing scenes that can occur on
earth, when a sin has been committed by one person against another, is, to forgive that sin; and
then according to the sublime and perfect pattern
of the Savior, pray to our Father in heaven to forgive him also. (*HC* 6:245)

They [those who have sinned] are fellow mortals,
we loved them once, shall we not encourage them
to reformation? We have not [yet] forgiven them
seventy times seven, as our Savior directed; perhaps we have not forgiven them once. There is
now a day of salvation to such as repent and
reform;—and they who repent not should be ca[st]
out from this society; yet we should woo them [to]
return to God, lest they escape not the damna[tion]
of hell! Where there is a mountain top, th[ere]

91

also a valley—we should act in all things on a proper medium to every immortal spirit. Notwithstanding the unworthy are among us, the virtuous should not, from self importance, grieve and oppress needlessly, those unfortunate ones. (*HC* 5:20)

Meekly persuade and urge everyone to forgive one another all their trespasses, offenses and sins, that they may work out their own salvation with fear and trembling. Brethren, bear and forbear one with another, for so the Lord does with us. Pray for your enemies in the Church and curse not your foes without: for vengeance is mine, saith the Lord, and I will repay. (*Discourses,* 213)

FRIENDSHIP

That person who never forsaketh his trust, should ever have the highest place of regard in our hearts, and our love should never fail, but increase more ¬d more, and this is my disposition and these ¬timents. (*Discourses,* 272)

ˈfully turneth away from his friends ¬ot easily forgiven. (*Discourses,*

The kindness of a man should never be forgotten. (*Discourses*, 272)

Friendship is one of the grand fundamental principles of "Mormonism"; [it is designed] to revolutionize and civilize the world, and cause wars and contentions to cease and men to become friends and brothers. Even the wolf and the lamb shall dwell together; the leopard shall lie down with the kid, the calf, the young lion and the fatling; and a little child shall lead them; the bear and the cow shall lie down together, and the sucking child shall play on the hole of the asp, and the weaned child shall play on the cockatrice's den; and they shall not hurt or destroy in all my holy mountains, saith the Lord of hosts. (*HC* 5:517)

GATHERING OF ISRAEL

[The] subject of the gathering . . . is a principle I esteem to be of the greatest importance to those who are looking for salvation in this generation, or in these, that may be called, "the latter times." All that the prophets that have written, from the days of righteous Abel, down to the last man that has left any testimony on record for our consideration, in speaking of the salvation of Israel in the last days, goes directly to show that it consists in the work of the gathering. (*HC* 2:260)

One of the most important points in the faith of the Church of the Latter-day Saints, through the fullness of the everlasting Gospel, is the gathering of Israel . . . that happy time when Jacob shall go up to the house of the Lord, to worship Him in spirit and in truth, to live in holiness. (*TPJS,* 92)

He who scattered Israel has promised to gather them; therefore inasmuch as you are to be instrumental in this great work, He will endow you with power, wisdom, might and intelligence, and every qualification necessary; while your minds will expand wider and wider, until you can circumscribe the earth and the heavens, reach forth into eternity, and contemplate the mighty acts of Jehovah in all their variety and glory. (*TPJS,* 166)

We believe in the literal gathering of Israel and in the restoration of the Ten Tribes. (A of F 1:10)

After this vision closed, the heavens were again opened unto us; and Moses appeared before us, and committed unto us the keys of the gathering of Israel from the four parts of the earth, and the leading of the ten tribes from the land of the north. (D&C 110:11)

GIFTS OF THE SPIRIT

We believe in the gift of tongues, prophecy, revelation, visions, healing, interpretation of tongues, and so forth. (A of F 1:7)

A man who has none of the gifts has no faith; and he deceives himself, if he supposes he has. Faith has been wanting, not only among the heathen, but in professed Christendom also, so that tongues, healings, prophecy, and prophets and apostles, and all the gifts and blessings have been wanting. (*TPJS*, 278)

All the gifts of the Spirit are not visible to the natural vision, or understanding of man; indeed very few of them are (*Discourses*, 105)

The greatest, the best, and the most useful gifts would be known nothing about by an observer. (*Commentary*, 162)

The gifts which follow them that believe and obey the Gospel, as tokens that the Lord is ever the same in His dealings with the humble lovers and followers of truth, began to be poured out among us, as in ancient days. (*HC* 1:322)

A man must have the discerning of spirits, as we before stated, to understand these things, and how is he to obtain this gift if there are no gifts of the Spirit? (*HC* 4:574)

The gifts of God are all useful in their place, but when they are applied to that which God does not intend, they prove an injury, a snare and a curse instead of a blessing. (*HC* 5:31–32)

If you will obey the gospel with honest hearts, I promise you in the name of the Lord that the gifts as promised by our Savior will follow you, and by this you may prove me to be a true servant of God. (*Encyclopedia,* 290)

GOD THE FATHER

We believe in God, the Eternal Father, and in His Son, Jesus Christ, and in the Holy Ghost. (A of F 1:1)

If men do not comprehend the character of God, they do not comprehend themselves. (*HC* 6:303)

God himself was once as we are now, and is an exalted man, and sits enthroned in yonder heavens! That is the great secret. If the veil were rent today, and the great God who holds this world in its orbit, and who upholds all worlds and all things by His power, was to make himself visible,—I say, if you were to see him today, you would see him like a man in form—like yourselves in all the person, image, and very form as a man; for Adam was created in the very fashion, image and likeness of God. (*HC* 6:305)

When we understand the character of God, and know how to come to Him, he begins to unfold the heavens to us, and to tell us all about it. When we are ready to come to him, he is ready to come to us. (*HC* 6:308)

We here observe that God is the only supreme governor and independent being in whom all fullness and perfection dwell; who is omnipotent, omnipresent, and omniscient; without beginning of days or end of life; and that in him every good gift and every good principle dwell; and that he is the Father of lights; in him the principle of faith dwells independently, and he is the object in whom the faith of all other rational and accountable beings centers for life and salvation. (*Lectures* 2:2)

The destinies of all people are in the hands of a just God, and He will do no injustice to any one. (*HC* 1:449)

Our heavenly Father is more liberal in His views, and boundless in His mercies and blessings, than we are ready to believe or receive; and, at the same time, is more terrible to the workers of iniquity, more awful in the executions of His punishments, and more ready to detect every false way, than we are apt to suppose Him to be. (*HC* 5:136)

The Father has a body of flesh and bones as tangible as man's. (D&C 130:22)

GOSSIP

The man who willeth to do well, we should extol his virtues, and speak not of his faults behind his back. (*Discourses,* 272)

There is no salvation in believing an evil report against our neighbor. (*Discourses,* 272)

GOVERNMENT

We believe in being subject to kings, presidents, rulers, and magistrates, in obeying, honoring, and sustaining the law. (A of F 1:12)

The Almighty is a lover of order and good government. (*HC* 4:339)

Governments were instituted of God for the benefit of man and . . . he holds men accountable for their acts in relation to them, either in making laws or administering them for the good and safety of society. (*Encyclopedia,* 304)

But meddle not with any man for his religion: all governments ought to permit every man to enjoy his religion unmolested. No man is authorized to take away life in consequence of difference of religion, which all laws and governments ought to tolerate and protect, right or wrong. Every man has a natural, and, in our country, a constitutional right to be a false prophet, as well as a true prophet. (*HC* 6:304)

Every government, from the creation to the present, when it ceased to be virtuous, and failed to execute justice, sooner or later has been overthrown. And without virtuous principles to actuate a government all care for justice is soon lost, and the only motive which prompts it to act is ambition and selfishness. (*HC* 2:11)

The government of the Almighty has always been very dissimilar to the governments of men, whether we refer to His religious government, or to the government of nations. The government of God has always tended to promote peace, unity, harmony, strength, and happiness; while that of man has been productive of confusion, disorder, weakness, and misery.

The greatest acts of the mighty men have been to depopulate nations and to overthrow kingdoms; and whilst they have exalted themselves and become glorious, it has been at the expense of the lives of the innocent, the blood of the oppressed, the moans of the widow, and the tears of the orphan. (*TPJS*, 254–55)

GRACE

We commend you to God and the word of His grace, which is able to make us wise unto salvation. (*TPJS*, 130)

And we know that justification through the grace of our Lord and Savior Jesus Christ is just and true;

And we know also, that sanctification through the grace of our Lord and Savior Jesus Christ is just and true, to all those who love and serve God with all their mights, minds, and strength. (D&C 20:30–31)

Grace for grace is a heavenly decree. (*HC* 6:427)

The doctrine that the Presbyterians and Methodists have quarreled so much about— once in grace, always in grace, or falling away from grace, I will say a word about. They are both wrong. Truth takes a road between them both, for while the Presbyterian says "once in grace, you cannot fall;" the Methodist says: "You can have grace today, fall from it to-morrow, next day have grace again; and so follow on, changing continually." But the doctrine of the Scriptures and the spirit of Elijah would show them both false, and take a road between them both; for, according to the Scripture, if men have received the good word of God, and tasted of the powers of the world to come, if they shall fall away, it is impossible to renew them again, seeing they have crucified the Son of God afresh, and put Him to an open shame; so there is a possibility of falling away; you could not be renewed again, and the power of Elijah cannot seal against this sin, for this a reserve made in the seals and power of the Priesthood. (*TPJS*, 350–51)

HAPPINESS

Happiness is the object and design of our existence, and will be the end thereof if we pursue the path that leads to it; and this path is virtue, uprightness, faithfulness, holiness, and keeping all the commandments of God. (*Writings,* 507)

The government of God has always tended to promote peace, unity, harmony, strength, and happiness; while that of man has been productive of confusion, disorder, weakness, and misery. (*TPJS,* 254)

HOLY GHOST

Neither is man capable to make [the works of the Lord] known, for they are only to be seen and understood by the power of the Holy Spirit, which God bestows on those who love him, and purify themselves before him. (D&C 76:116)

No man can receive the Holy Ghost without receiving revelations. The Holy Ghost is a revelator. (*HC* 6:58)

There is a difference between the Holy Ghost and the gift of the Holy Ghost. Cornelius received the Holy Ghost before he was baptized, which was the convincing power of God unto him of the truth of the Gospel, but he could not receive the gift of the Holy Ghost until after he was baptized. Had he not taken this sign or ordinance upon him, the Holy Ghost which convinced him of the truth of God, would have left him. (*HC* 4:555)

We believe in the gift of the Holy Ghost being enjoyed now, as much as it was in the Apostles' days; we believe that it [the gift of the Holy Ghost] is necessary to make and to organize the Priesthood, that no man can be called to fill any office in the ministry without it; we also believe in prophecy, in tongues, in visions, and in revelations, in gifts, and in healings; and that these things cannot be enjoyed without the gift of the Holy Ghost. . . .

We believe in it this gift of the Holy Ghost in all its fullness, and power, and greatness, and glory; but whilst we do this, we believe in it rationally, consistently, and scripturally, and not according to the wild vagaries, foolish notions and traditions of men. (*HC* 5:27)

I thank God that I have got this old book [the Bible]; but I thank him more for the gift of the Holy Ghost. I have got the oldest book in the world; but I have got the oldest book in my heart, even the gift of the Holy Ghost. (*HC* 6:308)

There are two Comforters spoken of. One is the Holy Ghost, the same as given on the day of Pentecost, and that all Saints receive after faith, repentance, and baptism. (*Discourses,* 41)

As we have noticed before, the great difficulty lies in the ignorance of the nature of spirits, of the laws by which they are governed, and the signs by which they may be known; if it requires the Spirit of God to know the things of God; and the spirit of the devil can only be unmasked through that medium, then it follows as a natural consequence that unless some person or persons have a communication, or revelation from God, unfolding to them the operation of the spirit, they must eternally remain ignorant of these principles. (*HC* 4:573–74)

HONESTY

Be honest; be men of truth and integrity; let your word be your bond. (*HC* 3:394)

Let honesty, and sobriety, and candor, and solemnity, and virtue, and pureness, and meekness, and simplicity crown our heads in every place; and in fine, become as little children, without malice, guile or hypocrisy. (*HC* 3:296)

HUMILITY

When pride shall fall and every aspiring mind be clothed with humility as with a garment, and selfishness give place to benevolence and charity, and a united determination to live by every word which proceedeth out of the mouth of the Lord is observable, then and not till then can peace, order, and love prevail. *(Commentary,* 204)

God exalts the humble, and debases the haughty. (*HC* 6:74)

We seek not gold or silver or this world's goods, nor honors nor the applause of men; but we seek to please him [God], and to do the will of him who hath power not only to destroy the body, but to cast the soul into hell! Ah! men should not attempt to steady the ark of God! (*Encyclopedia,* 331)

The true principle of honor in the Church of the Saints, that the more a man is exalted, the more humble he will be—if actuated by the Spirit of the Lord—seem[s] to have been overlooked. And the fact that the greatest is the least and servant of all, as said our Savior, [seems] never to have been thought of. (*Commentary,* 101)

INTELLIGENCE

There is a superior intelligence bestowed upon such as obeyed the Gospel with full purpose of heart. (*Discourses,* 225)

I therefore availed myself of this favorable opportunity to drop a few words upon this subject [of miracles], by way of advice, that they might improve their minds and cultivate their powers of intellect in a proper manner, that they might not incur the displeasure of heaven; that they should handle sacred things very sacredly, and with due deference to the opinions of others, and with an eye single to the glory of God. (*HC* 2:318)

After man was created, he was not left without intelligence or understanding, to wander in darkness and spend an existence in ignorance and doubt (on the great and important point which effected his happiness) as to the real fact by whom he was created, or unto whom he was amenable for his conduct. God conversed with him face to face. In his presence he was permitted to stand, and from his own mouth he was permitted to receive instruction. He heard his voice, walked before him and gazed upon his glory, while intelligence burst upon his understanding, and enabled him to give names to the vast assemblage of his Maker's works. (*Lectures* 2:18)

The Lord deals with this people as a tender parent with a child, communicating light and intelligence and the knowledge of his ways as they can bear it. (*TPJS,* 315)

Intelligence is eternal and exists upon a self-existent principle. It is a spirit from age to age and there is no creation about it. (*HC* 6:311)

The spirit or the intelligence of men are self-existent principles before the foundation [of] this earth. (*Commentary,* 40)

JESUS CHRIST

And we beheld the glory of the Son, on the right hand of the Father, and received of his fulness;

And saw the holy angels, and them who are sanctified before his throne, worshiping God, and the Lamb, who worship him forever and ever.

And now, after the many testimonies which have been given of him, this is the testimony, last of all, which we give of him: That he lives!

For we saw him, even on the right hand of God; and we heard the voice bearing record that he is the Only Begotten of the Father—

That by him, and through him, and of him, the worlds are and were created, and the inhabitants thereof are begotten sons and daughters unto God. (D&C 76: 20–24)

Christ [is] the head of the Church, the chief corner stone, the spiritual rock upon which the church was built, and the gates of hell shall not prevail against it. (*TPJS,* 329)

The Son, who was in the bosom of the Father, [is] a personage of tabernacle, made or fashioned like unto man, being in the form and likeness of man, or rather man was formed after his likeness and in his image; he is also the express image and likeness of the personage of the Father, possessing all the fullness of the Father, or the same fullness with the Father; being begotten of him, and ordained from before the foundation of the world to be a propitiation for the sins of all those who should believe on his name, and is called the Son because of the flesh, and descended in suffering below that which man can suffer; or, in other words, suffered greater sufferings, and was exposed to more powerful contradictions than any man can be. But, notwithstanding all this, he kept the law of God, and remained without sin, showing thereby that it is in the power of man to keep the law and remain also without sin; and also, that by him a righteous judgment might come upon all flesh, that all who walk not in the law of God may justly be condemned by the law, and have no excuse for their sins. And he being the Only Begotten of the Father, full of grace and truth, and having overcome, received a fullness of the glory of the Father, possessing the same mind with the Father, which mind is the Holy Spirit, that bears record of the Father and the Son. (*Encyclopedia,* 334–35)

None ever were perfect but Jesus; and why was he perfect? Because he was the Son of God, and had the fulness of the Spirit, and greater power than any man. But notwithstanding their vanity, men look forward with hope (because they are "subjected in hope") to the time of their deliverance. (*Discourses,* 43)

Who among all the Saints in these last days can consider himself as good as our Lord? Who is as perfect, who is as pure, and who as holy as he was? Are they to be found? He never transgressed or broke a commandment or law of heaven. No deceit was in his mouth, neither was guile found in his heart. And yet one that ate with him, who had often supped of the same cup, was the first to lift up his heel against him. Where is there one like him? He cannot be found on earth. Then why should his followers complain if from those whom they once called brethren, and considered in the nearest relation in the everlasting covenant, they should receive persecution? (*Commentary,* 127)

Salvation could not come to the world without the mediation of Jesus Christ. . . .

Jesus Christ is the heir of this Kingdom—the only begotten of the Father according to the flesh, and holds the keys over all this world. (*Encyclopedia,* 348–49)

The Savior has the words of eternal life. Nothing else can profit us. (*Discourses,* 272)

The scriptures inform us that Jesus said, as the Father hath power in himself, even so hath the Son power—to do what? Why, what the Father did. The answer is obvious—in a manner to lay down his body and take it up again. Jesus, what are you going to do? To lay down my life as my Father did, and take it up again. . . .

What did Jesus do? Why, I do the things I saw my Father do when worlds came rolling into existence. My Father worked out His kingdom with fear and trembling, and I must do the same; and when I get my kingdom, I shall present it to My Father, so that He may obtain kingdom upon kingdom, and it will exalt Him in glory. He will then take a higher exaltation, and I will take His place, and thereby become exalted myself. So that Jesus treads in the tracks of His Father, and inherits what God did before; and God is thus glorified and exalted in the salvation and exaltation of all His children. (*Encyclopedia,* 349)

Jesus Christ became a ministering spirit (while His body was lying in the sepulchre) to the spirits in prison, to fulfill an important part of His mission, without which He could not have perfected His work, or entered into His rest. After His resurrection He appeared as an angel to His disciples. . . .

Jesus Christ went in body after His resurrection, to minister to resurrected bodies. (*HC* 4;425)

So that after the testimony of the Scriptures on this point, the assurance is given by the Holy Ghost, bearing witness to those who obey Him, that Christ Himself has assuredly risen from the dead; and if He has risen from the dead, He will by His power, bring all men to stand before Him; for if He has risen from the dead the bands of the temporal death are broken that the grave has no victory. If then, the grave has no victory, those who keep the sayings of Jesus and obey His teachings have not only a promise of a resurrection from the dead, but an assurance of being admitted into His glorious kingdom; for, He Himself says, "Where I am, there shall also my servant be" (see John 12). (*TPJS,* 60–61)

Christ came according to the words of John, and He was greater than John, because He held the keys of the Melchisedek Priesthood and kingdom of God, and had before revealed the priesthood of Moses, yet Christ was baptized by John to fulfill all righteousness. (*HC* 5:258)

He laid down his life and took it up, same as his Father had done before. He did it as he was sent, to lay down his life and take it up again. (*Commentary,* 132)

JUDGMENT

And I continued and said, no man is capable of judging a matter, in council, unless his own heart is pure; and that we frequently are so filled with prejudice, or have a beam in our own eye, that we are not capable of passing right decisions. (*Discourses,* 290)

But while one portion of the human race is judging and condemning the other without mercy, the Great Parent of the universe looks upon the whole of the human family with a fatherly care and paternal regard; He views them as His offspring, and without any of those contracted feelings that influence the children of man, causes

"His sun to rise on the evil and on the good, and sendeth rain on the just and on the unjust." (*HC* 4:595)

[God] holds the reins of judgment in His hands; He is a wise Lawgiver, and will judge all men, not according to the narrow, contracted notions of men, but, "according to the deeds done in the body whether they be good or evil." . . . He will judge them, "not according to what they have not, but according to what they have," those who have lived without law, will be judged without law, and those who have a law, will by judged by that law. We need not doubt the wisdom and intelligence of the Great Jehovah; . . . and when the designs of God shall be made manifest, and the curtain of futurity be withdrawn, we shall all of us eventually have to confess that the Judge of all the earth has done right. (*HC* 4:595–96)

For they shall be judged according to their works, and every man shall receive according to his own works, his own dominion, in the mansions which are prepared. (D&C 76:111)

Our acts are recorded, and at a future day they will be laid before us, and if we should fail to judge right and injure our fellow-beings, they may there,

perhaps, condemn us; there they are of great consequence, and to me the consequence appears to
be of force, beyond anything which I am able to
express. Ask yourselves, brethren, how much you
have exercised yourselves in prayer since you
heard of this council; and if you are now prepared
to sit in council upon the soul of your brother.
(*HC* 2:26)

KNOWLEDGE

O may God give me learning, . . . and endue me
with qualifications to magnify His name while I
live. (*HC* 2:344)

As far as we degenerate from God, we descend to
the devil and lose knowledge, and without knowledge we cannot be saved. . . .

A man is saved no faster than he gets knowledge, for if he does not get knowledge, he will be
brought into captivity by some evil power in the
other world, as evil spirits will have more knowledge, and consequently more power than many
men who are on the earth. Hence it needs revelation to assist us, and give us knowledge of the
things of God. (*Encyclopedia,* 372–73)

Knowledge saves a man; and in the world of spirits no man can be exalted but by knowledge. So long as a man will not give heed to the commandments, he must abide without salvation. If a man has knowledge, he can be saved; although, if he has been guilty of great sins, he will be punished for them. But when he consents to obey the gospel, whether here or in the world of spirits, he is saved. (*HC* 6:314)

The exaltation and happiness of any community, goes hand in hand with the knowledge possessed by the people, when applied to laudable ends; whereupon we can exclaim like the wise man; righteousness exalteth a nation; for righteousness embraces knowledge and knowledge is power. (*Encyclopedia,* 373)

If we get puffed up by thinking that we have much knowledge, we are apt to get a contentious spirit, and correct knowledge is necessary to cast out that spirit.

The evil of being puffed up with correct (though useless) knowledge is not so great as the evil of contention. Knowledge does away with darkness, suspense and doubt; for these cannot exist where knowledge is. . . .

In knowledge there is power. God has more power than all other beings, because he has greater knowledge; and hence he knows how to subject all other beings to Him. He has power over all. (*TPJS,* 296)

It is not wisdom that we should have all knowledge at once presented before us; but that we should have a little at a time; then we can comprehend it. . . .

Add to your faith knowledge, etc. The principle of knowledge is the principle of salvation. This principle can be comprehended by the faithful and diligent; and every one that does not obtain knowledge sufficient to be saved will be condemned. The principle of salvation is given us through the knowledge of Jesus Christ. (*Discourses,* 202–03)

Knowledge is power; and the man who has the most knowledge has the greatest power. (*HC* 5:392)

Many . . . dishonor themselves and the Church, and bring persecution swiftly upon us, in consequence of their zeal without knowledge. (*HC* 2:394)

There are a great many wise men and women too in our midst who are too wise to be taught; therefore they must die in their ignorance, and in the resurrection they will find their mistake. Many seal up the door of heaven by saying, So far God may reveal and I will believe. (*HC* 5:424)

LAST DAYS/SECOND COMING

This messenger [Moroni] proclaimed himself to be an angel of God, sent to bring the joyful tidings that the covenant which God made with ancient Israel was at hand to be fulfilled, that the preparatory work for the second coming of the Messiah was speedily to commence; that the time was at hand for the Gospel in all its fullness to be preached in power, unto all nations that a people might be prepared for the Millennial reign. (*HC* 4:536–37)

When I contemplate the rapidity with which the great and glorious day of the coming of the Son of Man advances, when He shall come to receive His Saints unto Himself, where they shall dwell in His presence, and be crowned with glory and immortality; when I consider that soon the heavens are to be shaken, and the earth tremble and reel to and fro; and that the heavens are to be unfolded as a scroll when it is rolled up; and that every mountain and island are to flee away,

I cry out in my heart, What manner of persons ought we to be in all holy conversation and godliness! (*HC* 1:442)

The time is near when the sun will be darkened, and the moon turn to blood, and the stars fall from heaven, and the earth reel to and fro. . . . If we are not sanctified and gathered to the places God has appointed, . . . we must fall; we cannot stand; we cannot be saved; for God will gather out his Saints from the Gentiles, and then comes desolation and destruction, and none can escape except the pure in heart who are gathered. (*HC* 2:52.)

After others had spoken I spoke and explained concerning the uselessness of preaching to the world about great judgments, but rather to preach the simple Gospel. Explained concerning the coming of the Son of Man; also that it is a false idea that the Saints will escape all the judgments, whilst the wicked suffer; for all flesh is subject to suffer, and "the righteous shall hardly escape"; still many of the Saints will escape, for the just shall live by faith; yet many of the righteous shall fall a prey to disease, to pestilence, etc., by reason of the weakness of the flesh, and yet be saved in the Kingdom of God. So that it is an unhallowed principle to say that such and such have transgressed because they have been preyed upon by the disease or death, for all flesh is subject to death; and the Savior has said, "Judge not, lest ye be judged." (*HC* 4:11)

In the former days God sent His servants to fight; but in the last days, He has promised to fight the battle Himself. (*HC* 5:356)

I will prophesy that the signs of the coming of the Son of Man are already commenced. One pestilence will desolate after another. We shall soon have war and bloodshed. The moon will be turned into blood. I testify of these things, and that the coming of the Son of Man is even at your doors. If our souls and our bodies are not looking forth for the coming of the Son of Man; and after we are dead, if we are not looking forth, we shall be among those who are calling for the rocks to fall upon them.

The hearts of the children of men will have to be turned to the fathers, and the fathers to the children, living or dead, to prepare them for the coming of the Son of Man. If Elijah did not come, the whole earth would be smitten.

There will be here and there a stake [of Zion] for the gathering of the Saints. Some may have cried peace, but the Saints and the world will have little peace from henceforth. Let this not hinder us from going to the stakes; for God has told us to flee, not dally, or we shall be scattered, one here, and another there. (*HC* 3:390)

LIBERTY

The cause of human liberty is the cause of God. (Discourses, 273)

LOVE

To be justified before God we must love one another: we must overcome evil; we must visit the fatherless and the widow in their affliction, and we must keep ourselves unspotted from the world: for such virtues flow from the great fountain of pure religion. (*HC* 2:229)

Love is one of the chief characteristics of Deity, and ought to be manifested by those who aspire to be the sons of God. A man filled with the love of God, is not content with blessing his family alone, but ranges through the whole world, anxious to bless the whole human race. (*HC* 4:227)

Those who loved Him would do His will and work righteousness; and it is vain for men to say they love God, if they do not keep His commandments. (*HC* 4:258)

It is a time-honored adage that love begets love. Let us pour forth love—show forth our kindness unto all mankind, and the Lord will reward us with everlasting increase; cast our bread upon the waters and we shall receive it after many days, increased to a hundredfold. Friendship is like Brother Turley in his blacksmith shop welding iron to iron; it unites the human family with its happy influence. (*HC* 5:517)

MERCY

To every ordained member, and to all, we say, be merciful and you shall find mercy. (*Discourses,* 213)

There should be no license for sin, but mercy should go hand in hand with reproof. (*HC* 5:24)

Don't envy the finery and fleeting show of sinners, for they are in a miserable situation; but as far as you can, have mercy on them. (*HC* 4:607)

Inasmuch as long-suffering, patience, and mercy have ever characterized the dealings of our heavenly Father towards the humble and penitent, I feel disposed to copy the example, cherish the same principles, and by so doing be a savior to my fellow men. (*HC* 4:163)

There is never a time when the spirit is too old to approach God. All are within the reach of pardoning mercy, who have not committed the unpardonable sin, which hath no forgiveness. (*HC* 4:425)

MILLENNIUM

This [the Millennium] is the only thing that can bring about the "restitution of all things spoken of by all the holy Prophets since the world was"— "the dispensation of the fullness of times, when God shall gather together all things in one." Other attempts to promote universal peace and happiness in the human family have proved abortive; every effort has failed; every plan and design has fallen to the ground; it needs the wisdom of God, the intelligence of God, and the power of God to accomplish this. The world has had a fair trial for six thousand years; the Lord will try the seventh thousand Himself; "He whose right it is, will possess the kingdom, and reign until He has put all things under His feet;" iniquity will hide its hoary head, Satan will be bound, and the works of darkness destroyed; righteousness will be put to the line, and judgment to the plummet, and "he that fears the Lord will alone be exalted in that day." To bring about this state of things, there must of necessity be great confusion among the nations of the earth; "distress of nations with perplexity." (*HC* 5:64–65)

The battle of Gog and Magog will be after the millennium. The remnant of all the nations that fight against Jerusalem were commanded to go up to Jerusalem to worship in the millennium. (*HC* 5:298)

Christ and the resurrected Saints will reign over the earth during the thousand years. They will not probably dwell upon the earth, but will visit it when they please, or when it is necessary to govern it. There will be wicked men on the earth during the thousand years. The heathen nations who will not come up to worship will be visited with the judgments of God, and must eventually be destroyed from the earth. (*HC* 5:212)

Christians should cease wrangling and contending with each other, and cultivate the principles of union and friendship in their midst; and they will do it before the millennium can be ushered in and Christ takes possession of His kingdom. (*HC* 5:499)

MIRACLES

If you have any darkness, you have only to ask, and the darkness is removed. It is not necessary that miracle[s] should be wrought to remove darkness. Miracles are the fruits of faith. (*HC* 5:355)

Joseph commenced laying before him the coming forth of the work, and the first principles of the Gospel, when Mr. Hayden exclaimed, "O this is not the evidence I want, the evidence that I wish to have is a notable miracle; I want to see some powerful manifestation of the power of God, I want to see a notable miracle performed; and if you perform such a one, then I will believe with all my heart and soul, and will exert all my power and all my extensive influence to convince others; and if you will not perform a miracle of this kind, then I am your worst and bitterest enemy." "Well," said Joseph, "what will you have done? Will you be struck blind, or dumb? Will you be paralyzed, or will you have one hand withered?

Take your choice, choose which you please, and in the name of the Lord Jesus Christ it shall be done." "That is not the kind of miracle I want," said the preacher. "Then, sir," replied Joseph, "I can perform none, I am not going to bring any trouble upon any body else, sir, to convince you. I will tell you what you make me think of—the very first person who asked a sign of the Savior, for it is written, in the New Testament, that Satan came to the Savior in the desert, when he was hungry with forty days' fasting, and said, 'If you be the Son of God, command these stones to be made bread.' And now," said Joseph, "the children of the devil and his servants have been asking for signs ever since; and when the people in that day continued asking him for signs to prove the truth of the Gospel which he preached, the Savior replied, 'It is a wicked and an adulterous generation that seeketh a sign.'" (*JD* 2:326–27)

MISSIONARY WORK

After all that has been said, the greatest and most important duty is to preach the Gospel. (*HC* 2:478)

All are to preach the Gospel, by the power and influence of the Holy Ghost; and no man can preach the Gospel without the Holy Ghost. (*HC* 2:477)

When the Lord's anointed go forth to proclaim the word, bearing testimony to this generation, if they receive it they shall be blessed; but if not, the judgments of God will follow close upon them, until that city or that house which rejects them, shall be left desolate. (*HC* 2:418–19)

Let the Elders be exceedingly careful about unnecessarily disturbing and harrowing up the feelings of the people. Remember that your business is to preach the Gospel in all humility and meekness, and warn sinners to repent and come to Christ. (*TPJS*, 40)

Brethren, as stars of the ensign which is now set up for the benefit of all nations, you are to enlighten the world, you are to prepare the way for the people to come up to Zion; you are to instruct men how to receive the fulness of the Gospel, and the everlasting covenants, even them that were from the beginning; you are to carry the ark of safety before the wondering multitudes, without fear, entreating and beseeching all men to be saved; you are to set an example of meekness and humility before Saints and sinners, as did the Savior; and when reviled you are not to revile again; you are to

reason with men, as in days of old, to bear patiently and answer as the spirit of truth shall direct,
allowing all credit for every item of good. You are
to walk in the valley of humility, and pray for the
salvation of all. (*HC* 1:280)

NEW JERUSALEM

Righteousness and truth are to sweep the earth as
with a flood. And now, I ask, how righteousness
and truth are going to sweep the earth as with a
flood? I will answer. Men and angels are to be co-
workers in bringing to pass this great work, and
Zion is to be prepared, even a new Jerusalem, for
the elect that are to be gathered from the four
quarters of the earth, and to be established an
holy city, for the tabernacle of the Lord shall be
with them. (*HC* 2:260)

Now we learn from the Book of Mormon the very
identical continent and spot of land upon which
the New Jerusalem is to stand, and it must be
caught up according to the vision of John upon
the isle of Patmos.

Now many will feel disposed to say, that this
New Jerusalem spoken of, is the Jerusalem that
was built by the Jews on the eastern continent.
But you will see, from Revelation xxi:2, there was

a New Jerusalem coming down from God out of heaven, adorned as a bride for her husband; that after this, the Revelator was caught away in the Spirit, to a great and high mountain, and saw the great and holy city descending out of heaven from God. Now there are two cities spoken of here. . . . There is a New Jerusalem to be established on this continent, and also Jerusalem shall be rebuilt on the eastern continent (See Ether xiii:1–12). (*HC* 2:261–62)

We believe . . . that Zion (the New Jerusalem) will be built upon the American continent. (A of F 1:10)

OBEDIENCE

I made this my rule: *When the Lord commands, do it.* (*Discourses,* 273)

I have no doubt but that you will agree with me that men will be held accountable for the things which they have done and not for the things they have not, or that all the light and intelligence communicated to them from their beneficent creator, whether it is much or little, by the same they in justice will be judged, and that they are required to yield obedience and improve upon that and that only which is given, for man is not to live by bread alone but by every word that proceeds out of the mouth of God. (*Encyclopedia,* 1997, 448)

Therefore let your heart be comforted; live in strict obedience to the commandments of God, and walk humbly before Him, and He will exalt thee in His own due time. (*HC* 1:408)

In obedience there is joy and peace unspotted, unalloyed; and as God has designed our happiness—and the happiness of all His creatures, he never has—He never will institute an ordinance or give a commandment to His people that is not calculated in its nature to promote that happiness which He has designed, and which will not end in the greatest amount of good and glory to those who become the recipients of his law and ordinances. (*HC* 5:135)

Live in strict obedience to the commandments of God, and walk humbly before Him, and He will exalt thee in His own due time. (*HC* 1:408)

To get salvation we must not only do some things, but everything which God has commanded. Men may preach and practice everything except those things which God commands us to do, and will be damned at last. We may tithe mint and rue, and all manner of herbs, and still not obey the commandments of God. The object with me is to obey and teach others to obey God in just what He tells us to do. It mattereth not whether the principle is popular or unpopular, I will always maintain a true principle, even if I stand alone in it. (*HC* 6:223)

OPPOSITION

In relation to the kingdom of God, the devil always sets up his kingdom at the very same time in opposition to God. (*HC* 6:364)

It seems as though the adversary was aware, at a very early period of my life, that I was destined to prove a disturber and an annoyer of his kingdom; else why should the powers of darkness combine against me? Why the opposition and persecution that arose against me, almost in my infancy? (JS—H 1:20)

ORDINANCES

And if Abel was taught of the coming of the Son of God, was he not taught also of His ordinances?

We all admit that the Gospel has ordinances, and if so, had it not always ordinances, and were not its ordinances always the same? (*HC* 2:16)

[God] set the ordinances to be the same forever and ever, and set Adam to watch over them, to reveal them from heaven to man, or to send angels to reveal them. (*HC* 4:208)

Being born again, comes by the Spirit of God through ordinances. (*HC* 3:392)

All men who become heirs of God and joint-heirs with Jesus Christ will have to receive the fulness of the ordinances of his kingdom; and those who will not receive all the ordinances will come short of the fullness of that glory, if they do not lose the whole. (*HC* 5:424)

The question is frequently asked "Can we not be saved without going through with all those ordinances, &c.?" I would answer, No, not the fullness of salvation. Jesus said, "There are many mansions in my Father's house, and I will go and prepare a place for you." House here named should have been translated kingdom; and any person who is exalted to the highest mansion has to abide a celestial law, and the whole law too. (*HC* 6:184)

All the ordinances and duties that ever have been required by the Priesthood, under the directions and commandments of the Almighty in any of the dispensations, shall all be had in the last dispensation. (*HC* 4:210–11)

If a man gets a fullness of the priesthood of God, he has to get it in the same way that Jesus Christ obtained it, and that was by keeping all the commandments and obeying all the ordinances of the house of the Lord. (*HC* 5:424)

The order and ordinances of the kingdom were instituted by the priesthood in the Council of Heaven before the world was. (*Encyclopedia*, 459)

PATIENCE

Patience is heavenly. (*HC* 6:427)

Enlarge your souls towards each other . . . bear with each other's failings as an indulgent parent bears with the foibles of his children. (*TPJS*, 235)

In our patience we possess our souls. (*HC* 5:96)

Men or women could not be compelled into the kingdom of God, but must be dealt with in long-suffering, and at last we shall save them. (*HC* 5:24)

Let your diligence and your perseverance, and patience, and your works be redoubled; and you shall in no wise lose your reward. (*HC* 5:143)

PEACE

If the nation, a single state, community, or family ought to be grateful for anything, it is peace. Peace, lovely child of heaven. Peace, like light from the same great parent, gratifies, animates, and happifies the just and the unjust and is the very essence of happiness below and bliss above. He that does not strive with all his powers of body and mind, with all his influence at home and abroad, and to cause others to do so too, to seek peace and maintain it for his own benefit and convenience and for the honor of his state, nation, and country, has no claim on the clemency of man, nor should he be entitled to the friendship of woman or the protection of government. . . . But the peacemaker, Oh give ear to him! For the words of his mouth, and his doctrine, drop like the rain and distil as the dew. (*Commentary,* 81)

I never did harm any man since I was born in the world. My voice is always for peace. (*HC* 6:317)

Our motto, then, is Peace with all! If we have joy in the love of God, let us try to give a reason of that joy, which all the world cannot gainsay or resist. (*HC* 6:220)

If, then, we admit that God is the source of all wisdom and understanding, we must admit that by His direct inspiration He has taught man that law is necessary in order to govern and regulate His own immediate interest and welfare; for this reason, that law is beneficial to promote peace and happiness among men. (*TPJS*, 53–54)

PERFECTION

The nearer man approaches perfection, the clearer are his views, and the greater his enjoyments, till he has overcome the evils of his life and lost every desire for sin; and like the ancients, arrives at that point of faith where he is wrapped in the power and glory of his Maker, and is caught up to dwell with Him. But we consider that this is a station to which no man ever arrived in a moment: he must have been instructed in the government and laws of that kingdom by proper degrees, until his mind is capable in some measure of comprehending the propriety, justice, equality, and consistency of the same. (*HC* 2:8)

I advise all to go on to perfection, and search deeper and deeper into the mysteries of Godliness. (*Discourses,* 273)

And now, my dearly beloved brethren and sisters, let me assure you that these are principles in relation to the dead and the living that cannot be lightly passed over, as pertaining to our salvation. For their salvation is necessary and essential to our salvation, as Paul says concerning the fathers—that they without us cannot be made perfect—neither can we without our dead be made perfect. (D&C 128:15)

PERSECUTION

Persecution has not stopped the progress of truth, but has only added fuel to the flame, it has spread with increasing rapidity. (*HC* 4:540)

Nothing therefore can separate us from the love of God and fellowship one with another; and . . . every species of wickedness and cruelty practiced upon us will only tend to bind our hearts together and seal them together in love. (*HC* 3:290)

This one thing is sure, that they who will live godly in Christ Jesus, shall suffer persecution; and before their robes are made white in the blood of the Lamb, it is to be expected, according to John the Revelator, they will pass through great tribulation. (*HC* 1:449)

Those who cannot endure persecution, and stand in the day of affliction, cannot stand in the day when the Son of God shall burst the veil, and appear in all the glory of His Father, with all the holy angels. (*HC* 1:468)

PLAN OF SALVATION

At the first organization in heaven we were all present, and saw the Savior chosen and appointed and the plan of salvation made, and we sanctioned it. (*Encyclopedia*, 482)

But that man was not able himself to erect a system, or plan with power sufficient to free him from a destruction which awaited him, is evident from the fact that God, as before remarked, prepared a sacrifice in the gift of His own Son who should be sent in due time, to prepare a way, or open a door through which man might enter into the Lord's presence, whence he had been cast out for disobedience. (*HC* 2:15)

The great plan of salvation is a theme which ought to occupy our strict attention, and be regarded as one of heaven's best gifts to mankind. No consideration whatever ought to deter us from showing ourselves approved in the sight of God, according to His divine requirement. (*Commentary,* 114)

Who but those who have duly considered the condescension of the Father of our spirits, in providing a sacrifice for His creatures, a plan of redemption, a power of atonement, a scheme of salvation, having as its great objects, the bringing of men back into the presence of the King of heaven, crowning them in the celestial glory, and making them heirs with the Son to that inheritance which is incorruptible, undefiled, and which fadeth not away—who but such can realize the importance of a perfect walk before all men, and a diligence in calling upon all men to partake of these blessings? How indescribably glorious are these things to mankind! Of a truth they may be considered tidings of great joy to all people; and tidings, too, that ought to fill the earth and cheer the hearts of every one when sounded in his ears. (*HC* 2:5–6)

There is a way to release the spirits of the dead; that is by the power and authority of the Priesthood—by binding and loosing on earth. This doctrine appears glorious, inasmuch as it exhibits the greatness of divine compassion and benevolence in the extent of the plan of human salvation.

This glorious truth is well calculated to enlarge the understanding, and to sustain the soul under troubles, difficulties and distresses. (*HC* 4:425)

The great designs of God in relation to the salvation of the human family, are very little understood by the professedly wise and intelligent generation in which we live. Various and conflicting are the opinions of men concerning the plan of salvation, the requisitions of the Almighty, the necessary preparations for heaven, the state and condition of departed spirits, and the happiness or misery that is consequent upon the practice of righteousness and iniquity according to their several notions of virtue and vice. . . .

The great Jehovah contemplated the whole of the events connected with the earth, pertaining to the plan of salvation, before it rolled into existence, or ever "the morning stars sang together" for joy; the past, the present, and the future were and are, with Him, one eternal "now;" He knew

of the fall of Adam, the iniquities of the antedilu-
vians, of the depth of iniquity that would be connected with the human family, their weakness
and strength, their power and glory, apostasies,
their crimes, their righteousness and iniquity; He
comprehended the fall of man, and his redemption; He knew the plan of salvation and pointed
it out; He was acquainted with the situation of all
nations and with their destiny; He ordered all
things according to the council of His own will;
He knows the situation of both the living and the
dead, and has made ample provision for their
redemption, according to their several circumstances, and the laws of the kingdom of God,
whether in this world, or in the world to come.
(*Encyclopedia,* 483)

PRAYER

I urged the necessity of prayer, that the Spirit
might be given, that the things of the Spirit might
be judged thereby, because the carnal mind cannot discern the things of God. (*HC* 2:31)

Slack not your duties in your families, but call
upon God for his blessings upon you, and your
families—upon your flocks and herds, and all
that pertains to you—that you may have peace

and prosperity—and while you are doing this, "pray for the peace of Zion, for they shall prosper that love her." (*Encyclopedia,* 495–96)

The effectual prayers of the righteous avail much. (*HC* 6:303)

The best way to obtain truth and wisdom is not to ask it from books, but to go to God in prayer, and obtain divine teaching. (*HC* 4:425)

Seek to know God in your closets, call upon him in the fields. Follow the directions of the Book of Mormon, and pray over, and for your families, your cattle, your flocks, your herds, your corn, and all things that you possess; ask the blessing of God upon all your labors, and everything that you engage in. (*TPJS,* 254)

[In reply to the question, "Do you want a wicked man to pray for you?"] Yes. If the fervent, effectual prayer of the righteous availeth much, a wicked man may avail a little when praying for a righteous man. . . . The prayer of the wicked man may do a righteous man good when it does the one who prays no good. (*Commentary,* 199)

PRIDE

Pride goes before destruction, and a haughty spirit before a downfall. (*HC* 6:411)

Let [them] be humble, and not be exalted, and beware of pride, and not seek to excel one above another, but act for each other's good, and pray for one another, and honor our brother or make honorable mention of his name, and not backbite and devour our brother. (*HC* 3:383–84)

All men are naturally disposed to walk in their own paths as they are pointed out by their own fingers and are not willing to consider and walk in the path which is pointed out by another, saying, This is the way, walk ye in it, although he should be an unerring director, and the Lord his God sent him. (*Encyclopedia*, 501–502)

Let not any man publish his own righteousness, for others can see that for him; sooner let him confess his sins, and then he will be forgiven, and he will bring forth more fruit. When a corrupt man is chastised he gets angry and will not endure it. (*Discourses*, 132)

If there are any among you who aspire after their own aggrandizement, and seek their own opulence, while their brethren are groaning in poverty, and are under sore trials and temptations, they cannot be benefited by the intercession of the Holy Spirit, which maketh intercession for us day and night with groanings that cannot be uttered.

We ought at all times to be very careful that such highmindedness shall never have place in our hearts; but condescend to men of low estate, and with all long-suffering bear the infirmities of the weak. (*TPJS*, 143)

When confidence is restored, when pride shall fall, and every aspiring mind be clothed with humility as with a garment, and selfishness give place to benevolence and charity, and a united determination to live by every word which proceedeth out of the mouth of the Lord is observable, then, and not till then, can peace, order and love prevail. (*HC* 4:166)

PRIESTHOOD

There has been a chain of authority and power from Adam down to the present time. (*HC* 4:425)

How have we come at the Priesthood in the last days? It came down, down, in regular succession. Peter, James, and John had it given to them and they gave it to others. Christ is the Great High Priest; Adam next. Paul speaks of the Church coming to an innumerable company of angels—to God the Judge of all—the spirits of just men made perfect; to Jesus the Mediator of the new covenant. (*HC* 3:387–88)

A man can do nothing for himself unless God direct him in the right way; and the priesthood is for that purpose. (*Discourses*, 273)

If a man gets a fullness of the priesthood of God, he has to get it in the same way that Jesus Christ obtained it, and that was by keeping all the commandments and obeying all the ordinances of the house of the Lord. (*HC* 5:424)

The Priesthood is an everlasting principle, and existed with God from eternity, and will to eternity, without beginning of days or end of years. The keys have to be brought from heaven whenever the Gospel is sent. . . .

The Priesthood is everlasting. . . . Wherever the ordinances of the Gospel are administered, there is the Priesthood. (*Encyclopedia*, 504)

Its [the Melchizedek Priesthood's] institution was prior to "the foundation of this earth, or the morning stars sang together, or the Sons of God shouted for joy," and is the highest and holiest Priesthood, and is after the order of the Son of God, and all other Priesthoods are only parts, ramifications, powers and blessings belonging to the same, and are held, controlled, and directed by it. It is the channel through which the Almighty commenced revealing His glory at the beginning of the creation of this earth, and through which He has continued to reveal Himself to the children of men to the present time, and through which He will make known His purposes to the end of time. (*HC* 4:207)

[The Melchizedek Priesthood] is the channel through which all knowledge, doctrine, the plan of salvation, and every important matter is revealed from heaven. (*Encyclopedia*, 372)

The power, glory and blessings of the Priesthood could not continue with [all] those who received ordination, [but] only as their righteousness continued. For Cain also being authorized to offer sacrifice, but not offering it in righteousness, therefore he was cursed. It signifies, then, that the ordinances must be kept in the very way God has appointed; otherwise their Priesthood will prove a cursing instead of a blessing. (*Commentary*, 18)

On the subject of ordination, a few words are necessary. In many instances there has been too much haste in this thing, and the admonition of Paul has been too slightingly passed over, which says, "Lay hands suddenly upon no man." Some have been ordained to the ministry, and have never acted in that capacity, or magnified their calling at all. Such may expect to lose their appointment, except they awake and magnify their office. Let the Elders abroad be exceedingly careful upon this subject, and when they ordain a man to the holy ministry, let him be a faithful man, who is able to teach others also; that the cause of Christ suffer not. It is not the multitude of preachers that is to bring about the glorious millennium! but it is those who are "called, and chosen, and faithful." (*HC* 1:468)

PROPHECY

I met the quorums in the evening . . . and gave them instructions in relation to the spirit of prophecy, and called upon the congregation to speak, and not to fear to prophesy good concerning the Saints, for if you prophesy the falling of these hills and the rising of the valleys, the downfall of the enemies of Zion and the rising of the kingdom of God, it shall come to pass. Do not quench the Spirit, for the first one that opens his mouth shall receive the Spirit of prophecy. (*HC* 2:428)

No man is a minister of Jesus Christ, without being a Prophet. No man can be the minister of Jesus Christ, except he has the testimony of Jesus & this is the Spirit of Prophecy. (*The Words of Joseph Smith,* 10)

For the testimony of Jesus is the spirit of prophecy. (*Discourses,* 270)

We believe that a man must be called of God, by prophecy, and by the laying on of hands by those who are in authority, to preach the Gospel and administer in the ordinances thereof. (A of F 1:5)

The Lord once told me that if at any time I got into deep trouble and could see no way out of it, if I would prophesy in His name, he would fulfill my words. (*They Knew the Prophet,* 50)

The more sure word of prophecy means a man's knowing that he is sealed up unto eternal life, by revelation and the spirit of prophecy, through the power of the Holy Priesthood. (D&C 131:5)

PROPHETS

If any person should ask me if I were a prophet, I should not deny it, as that would give me the lie; for, according to John, the testimony of Jesus is the spirit of prophecy; therefore, if I profess to be a witness or teacher, and have not the spirit of prophecy, which is the testimony of Jesus, I must be a false witness; but if I be a true teacher and witness, I must possess the spirit of prophecy, and that constitutes a prophet; and any man who says he is a teacher or preacher of righteousness, and denies the spirit of prophecy, is a liar, and the truth is not in him; and by this key false teachers and imposters may be detected. (*HC* 5:215–216)

Wednesday, 8.—This morning, I read German, and visited with a brother and sister from Michigan, who thought that "a prophet is always a prophet;" but I told them that a prophet was a prophet only when he was acting as such. (*HC* 5:265)

A man would command his son to dig potatoes and saddle his horse, but before he had done either he would tell him to do something else. This is all considered right; but as soon as the Lord gives a commandment and revokes that decree and commands something else, then the Prophet is considered fallen. (*HC* 4:478)

The world always mistook false prophets for true ones, and those that were sent of God, they considered to be false prophets, and hence they killed, stoned, punished and imprisoned the true prophets, and these had to hide themselves "in deserts and dens, and caves of the earth," and though the most honorable men of the earth, they banished them from their society as vagabonds, whilst they cherished, honored and supported knaves, vagabonds, hypocrites, impostors, and the basest of men. (*HC* 4:574)

I am your servant, and it is only through the Holy Ghost that I can do you good. God is able to do His own work.

We do not present ourselves before you as anything but your humble servants, willing to spend and be spent in your service. (*HC* 5:355)

When a man goes about prophesying, and commands men to obey his teachings, he must either be a true or false prophet. False prophets always arise to oppose the true prophets and they will prophesy so very near the truth that they will deceive almost the very chosen ones. (*HC* 6:364)

RELIEF SOCIETY

You will receive instructions through the order of the Priesthood which God has established, through the medium of those appointed to lead, guide and direct the affairs of the Church in this last dispensation: and I now turn the key in your behalf in the name of the Lord, and this Society shall rejoice, and knowledge and intelligence shall flow down from this time henceforth; this is the beginning of better days to the poor and needy, who shall be made to rejoice and pour forth blessings on your heads. (*HC* 4:607)

The Church was never perfectly organized until the women were thus organized. (*Encyclopedia,* 538)

The best measure or principle to bring the poor to repentance is to administer to their wants. The Ladies' Relief Society is not only to relieve the poor, but to save souls. (*HC* 5:24–25)

This is a charitable Society, and according to your natures; it is natural for females to have feelings of charity and benevolence. You are now placed in a situation in which you can act according to those sympathies which God has planted in your bosoms. (*HC* 4:605)

If you live up to your privileges, the angels cannot be restrained from being your associates. . . . If this Society listen to the counsel of the Almighty, through the heads of the Church, they shall have power to command queens in their midst. (*HC* 4:605)

REPENTANCE

Repentance is a thing that cannot be trifled with every day. Daily transgression and daily repentance is not that which is pleasing in the sight of God. (*HC* 3:379)

You cannot go anywhere but where God can find you out. (*Discourses,* 272)

Christ said He came to call sinners to repentance, to save them. Christ was condemned by the self-righteous Jews because He took sinners into His society; He took them upon the principle that they repented of their sins. It is the object of this society to reform persons, not to take those that are corrupt and foster them in their wickedness; but if they repent, we are bound to take them, and by kindness sanctify and cleanse them from all unrighteousness by our influence in watching over them. (*HC* 5:23)

The Lord once told me that what I asked for I should have. I have been afraid to ask God to kill my enemies, lest some of them should, peradventure, repent. (*Discourses,* 273)

We should take warning and not wait for the death-bed to repent, as we see the infant taken away by death, so may the youth and middle aged, as well as the infant be suddenly called into eternity. Let this, then, prove as a warning to all not to procrastinate repentance, or wait till a death-bed for it is the will of God that man should repent and serve Him in health, and in the strength and power of his mind, in order to secure His blessing, and not wait until he is called to die. (*HC* 4:554)

Search your hearts, and see if you are like God. I have searched mine, and feel to repent of all my sins. (*Discourses,* 47)

And again, by way of commandment to the church concerning the manner of baptism—All those who humble themselves before God, and desire to be baptized, and come forth with broken hearts and contrite spirits, and witness before the church that they have truly repented of all their sins, and are willing to take upon them the name of Jesus Christ, having a determination to serve him to

the end, and truly manifest by their works that
they have received of the Spirit of Christ unto the
remission of their sins, shall be received by baptism into his church. (D&C 20:37)

RESTORATION

All things had under the authority of the
Priesthood at any former period, shall be had
again, bringing to pass the restoration spoken of
by the mouth of all the Holy Prophets. (*HC*
4:211)

It is in the order of heavenly things that God
should always send a new dispensation into the
world when men have apostatized from the truth
and lost the priesthood; but when men come out
and build upon other men's foundations, they do
it on their own responsibility, without authority
from God; and when the floods come and the
winds blow, their foundations will be found to be
sand, and their whole fabric will crumble to dust.
(*HC* 6:478–79)

The dispensation of the fullness of times will
bring to light the things that have been revealed
in all former dispensations; also other things that
have not been before revealed. (*HC* 4:426)

We are called to hold the keys of the mysteries of those things that have been kept hid from the foundation of the world until now. Some have tasted a little of these things, many of which are to be poured down from heaven upon the heads of babes; yea, upon the weak, obscure and despised ones of the earth. . . .

And now, brethren, after your tribulations, if you do these things, and exercise fervent prayer and faith in the sight of God always, He shall give unto you knowledge by His Holy Spirit, yea by the unspeakable gift of the Holy Ghost, that has not been revealed since the world was until now; which our forefathers have waited with anxious expectation to be revealed in the last times, with their minds were pointed to by the angels, as held in reserve for the fullness of their glory; a time to come in which nothing shall be withheld. (*HC* 3:296)

The work of the Lord in these last days, is one of vast magnitude and almost beyond the comprehension of mortals. Its glories are past description, and its grandeur unsurpassable. It is the theme which has animated the bosom of prophets and righteous men from the creation of the world down through every succeeding generation to the present time; and it is truly the dispensation of the fullness of times, when all things which are in Christ Jesus, whether in heaven or on the earth, shall be gathered together in Him, and when all things shall be restored, as spoken of by all the holy prophets since the world began; for in it will take place the glorious fulfillment of the promises made to the fathers, while the manifestations of the power of the Most High will be great, glorious, and sublime. (*Discourses,* 235)

Here, then, beloved brethren, is a work to engage in worthy of archangels—a work which will cast into the shade the things which have been heretofore accomplished; a work which kings and prophets and righteous men in former ages have sought, expected, and earnestly desired to see, but died without the sight; and well will it be for those who shall aid in carrying into effect the mighty operations of Jehovah. (*HC* 4:187)

The above clouds of darkness [anti-Mormon writings] have long been beating like mountain waves upon the immovable rock of the Church of the Latter-day Saints; and notwithstanding all this, the mustard seed is still towering its lofty branches, higher and higher, and extending itself wider and wider; and the chariot wheels of the Kingdom are still rolling on, impelled by the mighty arm of Jehovah; and in spite of all opposition, will still roll on, until His words are all fulfilled. (*Encyclopedia,* 553)

RESURRECTION

Now I understand by this quotation [Moses 7:62], that God clearly manifested to Enoch the redemption which He prepared, by offering the Messiah as a Lamb slain from before the foundation of the world; and by virtue of the same, the glorious resurrection of the Savior, and the resurrection of all the human family, even a resurrection of their corporeal bodies, is brought to pass. (*HC* 2:260)

They who obtain a glorious resurrection from the dead, are exalted far above principalities, powers, thrones, dominions and angels, and are expressly declared to be heirs of God and joint heirs with Jesus Christ, all having eternal power. (*HC* 6:478)

The doctrine of the resurrection of the dead and the eternal judgment are necessary to preach among the first principles of the Gospel of Jesus Christ. (*HC* 3:379)

Speaking of the resurrection of the dead, concerning those who shall hear the voice of the Son of Man:

And shall come forth; they who have done good in the resurrection of the just; and they who have done evil, in the resurrection of the unjust. (D&C 76:16–17)

All men will be raised from the grave by the power of God, having spirit in their bodies and not blood. (*Discourses,* 273)

Whatever principle of intelligence we attain unto in this life, it will rise with us in the resurrection. (D&C 130:18)

REVELATION

The Spirit of Revelation is in connection with these blessings. A person may profit by noticing the first intimation of the spirit of revelation; for instance, when you feel pure intelligence flowing into you, it may give you sudden strokes of ideas, so that by noticing it, you may find it fulfilled the same day or soon; (i.e.) those things that were presented unto your minds by the Spirit of God, will come to pass; and thus by learning the Spirit of God and understanding it, you may grow into the principle of revelation, until you become perfect in Christ Jesus. (*HC* 3:381)

It is also the privilege of any officer in this Church to obtain revelations, so far as relates to his particular calling and duty in the Church. All are bound by the principles of virtue and happiness, but one great privilege of the Priesthood is to obtain revelations of the mind and will of God. It is also the privilege of the Melchizedek Priesthood, to reprove, rebuke, and admonish, as well as to receive revelation. (*HC* 2:477)

I contend that if one man cannot understand these things but by the Spirit of God, ten thousand men cannot; it is alike out of the reach of the wisdom of the learned, the tongue of the eloquent, the power of the mighty. And we shall at last have to come to this conclusion, whatever we may think of revelation, that without it we can neither know nor understand anything of God, or the devil; and however unwilling the world may be to acknowledge this principle, it is evident from the multifarious creeds and notions concerning this matter that they understand nothing of this principle, and it is equally as plain that without a divine communication they must remain in ignorance. (*HC* 4:574)

The plea of many in this day is, that we have no right to receive revelations; but if we do not get revelations, we do not have the oracles of God; and if they have not the oracles of God, they are not the people of God. But say you, What will become of the world, or the various professors of religion who do not believe in revelation and the oracles of God as continued to His Church in all ages of the world, when He has a people on earth? I tell you, in the name of Jesus Christ, they will be damned; and when you get into the eternal world, you will find it will be so, they cannot escape the damnation of hell. (*HC* 5:257)

Jesus in His teachings says, "Upon this rock I will build my Church, and the gates of hell shall not prevail against it." What rock? Revelation. (*HC* 5:258)

God said, "Thou shalt not kill"; at another time he said "Thou shalt utterly destroy." This is the principle on which the government of heaven is conducted—by revelation adapted to the circumstances in which the children of the kingdom are placed. Whatever God requires is right, no matter what it is, although we may not see the reason thereof till long after the events transpire. If we seek first the kingdom of God, all good things will be added. (*Discourses*, 70)

RIGHTEOUSNESS

Righteousness must be the aim of the Saints in all things, and when the covenants are published, they will learn that great things must be expected from them. Do good and work righteousness with an eye single to the glory of God. (*HC* 2:229)

Brethren, from henceforth, let truth and righteousness prevail and abound in you; and in all
things be temperate; abstain from drunkenness,
and from swearing, and from all profane language, and from everything which is unrighteous
or unholy; also from enmity, and hatred, and covetousness, and from every unholy desire. Be honest one with another, for it seems that some have
come short of these things, and some have been
uncharitable, and have manifested greediness
because of their debts towards those who have
been persecuted and dragged about with chains
without cause, and imprisoned. Such characters
God hates—and they shall have their turn of sorrow in the rolling of the great wheel, for it rolleth
and none can hinder. (*TPJS*, 130)

Finally, in these critical times, be careful; call on
the Lord day and night; beware of pride; . . .
Awake to righteousness, and sin not; let your light
shine, and show yourselves workmen that need
not be ashamed, rightly dividing the word of
truth. Apply yourselves diligently to study, that
your minds may be stored with all necessary
information. (*HC* 1:468–69)

It is for us to be righteous, that we may be wise
and understand; for none of the wicked shall
understand; but the wise shall understand, and

they that turn many to righteousness shall shine as the stars for ever and ever. (*HC* 5:65)

The praise of men, or the honor of this world, is of no benefit; but if a man is respected in his calling, and considered to be a man of righteousness, the truth may have an influence, many times, by which means they may teach the gospel with success, and lead men unto the kingdom of heaven. (*Encyclopedia*, 582)

Righteousness is not that which men esteem holiness. That which the world call righteousness I have not any regard for. To be righteous is to be just and merciful. (*Commentary*, 83)

SABBATH DAY

They will, therefore, knowing that the Lord will suddenly come to His temple, do their part in preparing the way, by observing the Sabbath day, and keeping it holy; by teaching their children the Gospel, and teaching them to pray; by avoiding extremes in all matters; by shunning every appearance of evil. (*HC* 1:276)

SACRIFICE

Let us here observe, that a religion that does not require the sacrifice of all things never has power sufficient to produce the faith necessary unto life and salvation; for, from the first existence of man, the faith necessary unto the enjoyment of life and salvation never could be obtained without the sacrifice of all earthly things. It was through this sacrifice, and this only, that God has ordained that men should enjoy eternal life; and it is through the medium of the sacrifice of all earthly things that men do actually know that they are doing the things that are well pleasing in the sight of God. When a man has offered in sacrifice all that he has for the truth's sake, not even withholding his life, and believing before God that he has been called to make this sacrifice because he seeks to do his will, he does know, most assuredly, that God does and will accept his sacrifice and offering, and that he has not, nor will not seek his face in vain. Under these circumstances, then, he can obtain the faith necessary for him to lay hold on eternal life. (*Lectures* 6:7)

Never since the foundation of this Church was laid, have we seen manifested a greater willingness to comply with the requisitions of Jehovah, a more ardent desire to do the will of God, more strenuous exertions used, or greater sacrifices made than there have been since the Lord said, "Let the Temple be built by the tithing of my people." (*TPJS*, 237)

The sacrifice required of Abraham in the offering up of Isaac, shows that if a man would attain to the keys of the kingdom of an endless life, he must sacrifice all things. (*HC* 5:555)

Oh, brethren, give up all to God; forsake all for Christ's sake. (*Encyclopedia*, 139)

SALVATION

The great designs of God in relation to the salvation of the human family, are very little understood by the professedly wise and intelligent generation in which we live. (*HC* 4:595)

It is not all to be comprehended in this world; it will be a great work to learn our salvation and exaltation even beyond the grave. (*Discourses*, 342)

If men would acquire salvation, they have got to be subject, before they leave this world, to certain rules and principles, which were fixed by an unalterable decree before the world was. (*HC* 6:50–51)

I will walk through the gates of heaven, and claim what I seal and those that follow me and my counsel. (*Discourses,* 273)

Perhaps there are principles here that few men have thought of. No person can have this salvation except through a tabernacle. (*TPJS,* 306)

Salvation cannot come without revelation; it is in vain for anyone to minister without it . . . Men of the present time testify of heaven and hell, and have never seen either; and I will say that no man knows these things without this. (*Discourses,* 67)

Salvation is nothing more nor less than to triumph over all our enemies and put them under our feet. And when we have power to put all enemies under our feet in this world, and a knowledge to triumph over all evil spirits in the world to come, then we are saved, as in the case of Jesus, who was to reign until He had put all enemies under His feet, and the last enemy was death. (*HC* 5:387–88)

SCRIPTURES

I pray that the Lord may enable you to treasure these things in your mind, for I know that His Spirit will bear testimony to all who seek diligently after knowledge from Him. I hope you will search the Scriptures to see whether these things are not also consistent with those things which the ancient Prophets and Apostles have written. (*HC* 1:442)

Who is it that writes these Scriptures? Not the men of the world or mere casual observers, but the apostles—men who knew one gift from another, and of course were capable of writing about it; if we had the testimony of the scribes and Pharisees concerning the outpouring of the Spirit on the day of Pentecost, they would have told us that it was no gift, but that the people were "drunken with new wine," and we shall finally have to come to the same conclusion that Paul did—"No man knows the things of God but by the Spirit of God." (*Discourses,* 102–3)

Now taking it for granted that the scriptures say what they mean, and mean what they say, we have sufficient grounds to go on and prove from the bible that the gospel has always been the same; the ordinances to fulfil its requirements, the same; and the officers to officiate, the same; and the signs and fruits resulting from the promises, the same. (*Encyclopedia,* 614)

O ye Twelve! and all Saints! profit by this important *Key*—that in all your trials, troubles, temptations, afflictions, bonds, imprisonments and death, see to it, that you do not betray heaven; . . . that you do not betray the revelations of God, whether in the Bible, Book of Mormon, or Doctrine and Covenants, or any other that ever was or ever will be given and revealed unto man in this world or that which is to come. Yea, in all your kicking and flounderings, see to it that you do not this thing, lest innocent blood be found upon your skirts, and you go down to hell. (*HC* 3:385)

Mankind verily say that the scriptures are with them. Search the scriptures, for they testify of things that these apostates would gravely pronounce blasphemy. (*HC* 6:474)

I have a key by which I understand the scriptures. I enquire, what was the question which drew out the answer, or caused Jesus to utter the parable? . . . To ascertain its meaning, we must dig up the root and ascertain what it was that drew the saying out of Jesus. (*TPJS*, 285)

SERVICE

Any service we can do the state at any time will be cheerfully done, for our ambition is to be serviceable to our country. (*TPJS*, 262)

I always feel glad to do all I can for individuals. (*Encyclopedia,* 631)

Let your labors be mostly confined to those around you, in the circle of your own acquaintance, as far as knowledge is concerned, it may extend to all the world; but your administering should be confined to the circle of your immediate acquaintance. (*HC* 4:607)

We pronounce the blessings of heaven upon the heads of the Saints who seek to serve God with undivided hearts, in the name of Jesus Christ. (*HC* 3:305)

SIN

If men sin wilfully after they have received the knowledge of the truth, there remaineth no more sacrifice for sin, but a certain fearful looking for of judgment and fiery indignation to come, which shall devour these adversaries. For he who despised Moses' law died without mercy under two or three witnesses. Of how much more severe punishment suppose ye, shall he be thought worthy, who hath sold his brother, and denied the new and everlasting covenant by which he was sanctified, calling it an unholy thing, and doing despite to the Spirit of grace. (*HC* 3:232)

Nothing is so much calculated to lead people to forsake sin as to take them by the hand, and watch over them with tenderness. When persons manifest the least kindness and love to me, O what power it has over my mind, while the opposite course has a tendency to harrow up all the harsh feelings and depress the human mind. (*HC* 5:23–24)

Our Savior says, that all manner of sin and blasphemy shall be forgiven men wherewith they shall blaspheme; but the blasphemy against the Holy Ghost shall not be forgiven, neither in this world, nor in the world to come, evidently showing that there are sins which may be forgiven in the world to come, although the sin of blasphemy [against the Holy Ghost] cannot be forgiven. (*HC* 4:596)

TEMPLES

In order to erect the Temple of the Lord, great exertions will be required on the part of the Saints, so that they may build a house which shall be accepted by the Almighty, and in which His power and glory shall be manifested. (*HC* 4:273)

The Church is not fully organized, in its proper order, and cannot be, until the Temple is completed, where places will be provided for the administration of the ordinances of the Priesthood. (*HC* 4:603)

Behold, the great day of the Lord is at hand; . . . and he shall purify the sons of Levi, and purge them as gold and silver, that they may offer unto the Lord an offering in righteousness. Let us, therefore, as a church and a people, and as Latter-day Saints, offer unto the Lord an offering in righteousness; and let us present in his holy temple, when it is finished, a book containing the records of our dead, which shall be worthy of all acceptation. (D&C 128:24)

Go to and finish the temple, and God will fill it with power, and you will then receive more knowledge concerning this priesthood. (*HC* 5:555)

Believing the time has now come, when it is necessary to erect a house of prayer, a house of order, a house for the worship of our God, where the ordinances can be attended to agreeably to His divine will, in this region of country—to accomplish which, considerable exertion must be made, and means will be required—and as the work must be hastened in righteousness, it behooves the Saints to weigh the importance of these things, in their minds, in all their bearings, and then take such steps as are necessary to carry them into operation; and arming themselves with courage, resolve to do all they can, and feel themselves as much interested as though the whole labor depended on themselves alone. By so doing they will emulate the glorious deeds of the fathers, and secure the blessings of heaven upon themselves and their posterity to the latest generation.

To those who feel thus interested, and can assist in this great work, we say, let them come to this place; by so doing they will . . . assist in the rolling on of the Kingdom. (*HC* 4:186)

The Lord has an established law in relation to the matter: there must be a particular spot for the salvation of our dead. I verily believe there will be a place, and hence men who want to save their dead can come and bring their families, do their work by being baptized and attending to the other ordinances for their dead, and then may go back again to live and wait till they go to receive their reward. (*HC* 6:319)

Some say it is better to give to the poor than to build the Temple. The building of the Temple has sustained the poor who were driven from Missouri, and kept them from starving; and it has been the best means for this object which could be devised.

Oh, all ye rich men of the Latter-day Saints from abroad, I would invite you to bring up some of your money—your gold, your silver, and your precious things, and give to the Temple. (*HC* 6:58–59)

TESTIMONY

His Spirit will bear testimony to all who seek diligently after knowledge from Him. (*HC* 1:442)

No man can be a minister of Jesus Christ except he has the testimony of Jesus; and this is the spirit of prophecy. Whenever salvation has been administered, it has been by testimony. (*HC* 3:389–90)

TRUTH

The Standard of Truth has been erected; no unhallowed hand can stop the work from progressing; persecutions may rage, mobs may combine, armies may assemble, calumny may defame, but the truth of God will go forth boldly, nobly, and independent, till it has penetrated every continent, visited every clime, swept every country, and sounded in every ear, till the purposes of God shall be accomplished, and the Great Jehovah shall say the work is done. (*HC* 4:540)

One truth revealed from heaven is worth all the sectarian notions in existence. (*Discourses,* 61)

Truth is "Mormonism." God is the author of it. He is our shield. It is by Him we received our birth. (*HC* 3:297)

The doctrine of the Latter-day Saints is truth. . . . Now, sir, you may think that it is a broad assertion that it is truth; but sir, the first and fundamental principle of our holy religion is that we believe that we have a right to embrace all and every item of truth, without limitation or without being circumscribed or prohibited by the creeds or superstitious notions of men. (*Encyclopedia,* 684)

Truth, remember, is hard and severe against all iniquity and wickedness. (*HC* 1:326)

We believe in . . . the final triumph of truth. (*Discourses,* 272)

Prejudice, with its attendant train of evil, is giving way before the force of truth, whose benign rays are penetrating the nations afar off. (*HC* 4:336)

We don't ask any people to throw away any good they have got; we only ask them to come and get more. What if all the world should embrace this Gospel? They would then see eye to eye, and the blessings of God would be poured out upon the people, which is the desire of my whole soul. (*TPJS*, 283)

One of the grand fundamental principles of "Mormonism" is to receive truth, let it come from whence it may.

. . . If by the principles of truth I succeed in uniting men of all denominations in the bonds of love, shall I not have attained a good object?

If I esteem mankind to be in error, shall I bear them down? No. I will lift them up, and in their own way too, if I cannot persuade them my way is better; and I will not seek to compel any man to believe as I do, only by the force of reasoning, for truth will cut its own way. (*Encyclopedia*, 685)

I cannot believe in any of the creeds of the different denominations, because they all have some things in them I cannot subscribe to, though all of them have some truth. I want to come up into the presence of God, and learn all things; but the creeds set up stakes, and say, "Hitherto shalt thou come, and no further"; which I cannot subscribe to. (*TPJS*, 338)

Truth carries its own influence and recommends itself. (*Encyclopedia*, 686)

UNITY

Unity is strength. "How pleasing it is for brethren to dwell together in unity!" Let the Saints of the Most High ever cultivate this principle, and the most glorious blessings must result, not only to them individually, but to the whole Church—the order of the kingdom will be maintained, its officers respected, and its requirements readily and cheerfully obeyed. (*HC* 4:227)

Now, let me say once for all, like the Psalmist of old, "How good and how pleasant it is for brethren to dwell together in unity." . . . Unity is power. (*HC* 6:70)

VIRTUE

In order to do this [serve the Lord effectively], he [a man] and all his house must be virtuous, and must shun the very appearance of evil. (*HC* 3:231)

Be virtuous and pure; be men of integrity and truth; keep the commandments of God; and then you will be able more perfectly to understand the difference between right and wrong—between the things of God and the things of men; and your path will be like that of the just, which shineth brighter and brighter unto the perfect day. (*HC* 5:31)

Truth, honor, virtue and innocence will eventually come out triumphant. (*HC* 3:292)

Truth, virtue, and honor, combined with energy and industry, pave the way to exaltation, glory and bliss. (*HC* 6:425)

WICKEDNESS

This generation is as corrupt as the generation of the Jews that crucified Christ; and if He were here to-day, and should preach the same doctrine He did then, they would put Him to death. (*HC* 6:58)

WISDOM

A man of God should be endowed with wisdom, knowledge, and understanding, in order to teach and lead the people of God. (*HC* 5:426)

And do thou grant, Holy Father, that all those who shall worship in this house may be taught words of wisdom out of the best books, and that they may seek learning even by study, and also by faith, as thou hast said. (D&C 109:14)

WORSHIP

We can only live by worshiping our God; all must do it for themselves; none can do it for another. (*HC* 5:24)

We claim the privilege of worshiping Almighty God according to the dictates of our own conscience, and allow all men the same privilege, let them worship how, where, or what they may. (A of F 1:11)

Our affections should be placed upon God and his work more intensely than upon our fellow beings. (*Discourses,* 273)

ZEAL

Finally, as one that greatly desires the salvation of men, let me remind you all to strive with godly zeal for virtue, holiness, and the commandments of the Lord. Be good, be wise, be just, be liberal. (*HC* 5:417)

Our children will rise up and call us blessed; and generations yet unborn will dwell with peculiar delight upon the scenes that we have passed through, the privations that we have endured; the untiring zeal that we have manifested; the all but insurmountable difficulties that we have overcome in laying the foundation of a work that brought about the glory and blessing which they will realize; . . . a work that is destined to bring about the destruction of the powers of darkness, the renovation of the earth, the glory of God, and the salvation of the human family. (*HC* 4:610)

Many . . . dishonor themselves and the Church, and bring persecution swiftly upon us, in consequence of their zeal without knowledge. (*HC* 2:394)

ZION

In regard to the building up of Zion, it has to be done by the counsel of Jehovah, by the revelations of heaven; and we should feel to say, "if the Lord go not with us, carry us not up hence." . . . We are trying here to gird up our loins, and purge from our midst the workers of iniquity; and we hope that when our brethren arrive from abroad, they will assist us to roll forth this good work, and to accomplish this great design, that "Zion may be built up in righteousness; and all nations flock to her standard;" that as God's people, under His direction, and obedient to His law, we may grow up in righteousness and truth; that when His purposes shall be accomplished, we may receive an inheritance among those that are sanctified. (*HC* 5:65–66)

The Lord wants the wheat and tares to grow together; for Zion must be redeemed with judgment, and her converts with righteousness. (*HC* 2:228)

The city of Zion spoken of by David, in the one hundred and second Psalm, will be built upon the land of America, "And the ransomed of the Lord shall return, and come to Zion with songs and everlasting joy upon their heads" (Isaiah xxxv:10); and then they will be delivered from the overflowing scourge that shall pass through the land. But Judah shall obtain deliverance at Jerusalem. . . . The Good Shepherd will put forth His own sheep, and lead them out from all nations where they have been scattered in a cloudy and dark day, to Zion, and to Jerusalem. (*HC* 1:315)

The Lord will have a place whence His word will go forth, in these last days, in purity; for if Zion will not purify herself, so as to be approved of in all things, in His sight, He will seek another people; for His work will go on until Israel is gathered, and they who will not hear His voice, must expect to feel His wrath. (*HC* 1:316)

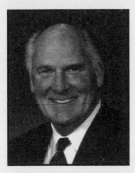

ED PINEGAR is a retired dentist and long-time teacher of early-morning seminary and religion classes at Brigham Young University. He teaches at the Joseph Smith Academy and has served as a mission president in England and at the Missionary Training Center in Provo, Utah. He has been a bishop and a stake president and is a temple sealer. Ed and his wife, Patricia, have eight children, thirty-five grandchildren, and five great-grandchildren and reside in Orem, Utah.